DEREK WALCOTT

Selected Poems

Derek Walcott was born in St. Lucia in 1930. He is the author of thirteen collections of poetry, seven collections of plays, and a book of essays. He received the Nobel Prize in Literature in 1992.

SELECTED POEMS

Selected Poems

DEREK WALCOTT

EDITED BY EDWARD BAUGH

FARRAR, STRAUS AND GIROUX

NEW YORK

FARRAR, STRAUS AND GIROUX
18 West 18th Street, New York 10011

The Library of Congress has cataloged the
hardcover edition as follows:
Walcott, Derek.
   [Poems. Selections]
   Selected poems / Derek Walcott; edited by Edward
Baugh.— 1st ed.
      p. cm.
   ISBN-13: 978-0-374-26066-8 (alk. paper)
   ISBN-10: 0-374-26066-4 (alk. paper)
   I. Baugh, Edward.   II. Title.

PR9272.9.W3A6 2007
811'.54—dc22

2006026944

Paperback ISBN-13: 978-0-374-53111-9
Paperback ISBN-10: 0-374-53111-0

Designed by Gretchen Achilles

www.fsgbooks.com

1 3 5 7 9 10 8 6 4 2

CONTENTS

Introduction *by Edward Baugh*   xi

From
IN A GREEN NIGHT: POEMS 1948–1960 (1962)

Prelude	3
As John to Patmos	4
A City's Death by Fire	5
A Far Cry from Africa	6
Ruins of a Great House	7
Tales of the Islands	9
Return to D'Ennery; Rain	14
A Letter from Brooklyn	16
Islands	18

From
THE CASTAWAY AND OTHER POEMS (1965)

The Castaway	21
Tarpon	23
The Flock	25
Laventille	27
The Almond Trees	31
Verandah	33
Crusoe's Island	35
Codicil	39

From
THE GULF AND OTHER POEMS (1969)

Mass Man	43
Homage to Edward Thomas	44

The Gulf   45
Blues   49
Air   51
Landfall, Grenada   53
Homecoming: Anse La Raye   54
Nearing Forty   56

From

ANOTHER LIFE (1973)

Chapter 1
   I ("Verandahs, where the pages of the sea")   61
   II ("In its dimension the drawing could not trace")   63
Chapter 2
   II ("Maman, / only on Sundays was the Singer silent")   65
   III ("Old house, old woman, old room")   66
Chapter 7
   II ("About the August of my fourteenth year")   69
   III ("Our father, / who floated in the vaults of Michelangelo")   70
   IV ("Noon, / and its sacred water sprinkles")   71
   V ("Who could tell, in 'the crossing of that pair' ")   71
Chapter 9
   I ("There are already, invisible on canvas")   72
   II ("Where did I fail? I could draw")   75
Chapter 14 ("When the oil green water glows but doesn't catch")   77
Chapter 20 ("Smug, behind glass, we watch the passengers")   81
Chapter 22 ("Miasma, acedia, the enervations of damp")   87

From

SEA GRAPES (1976)

Sea Grapes   97
Adam's Song   98
The Cloud   99
Parades, Parades   100
The Bright Field   102

Sainte Lucie 103
Volcano 116
Sea Canes 118
Midsummer, Tobago 119
Oddjob, a Bull Terrier 120
To Return to the Trees 122

From

THE STAR-APPLE KINGDOM (1979)

The Schooner *Flight* 127
  1. *Adios, Carenage* 127
  3. *Shabine Leaves the Republic* 129
  4. *The* Flight, *Passing Blanchisseuse* 130
  5. *Shabine Encounters the Middle Passage* 130
  6. *The Sailor Sings Back to the Casuarinas* 131
  7. *The* Flight *Anchors in Castries Harbour* 132
  8. *Fight with the Crew* 133
  10. *Out of the Depths* 133
  11. *After the Storm* 135
The Sea Is History 137
The Saddhu of Couva 140
Forest of Europe 142

From

THE FORTUNATE TRAVELLER (1981)

Piano Practice 147
Europa 149
The Spoiler's Return 150
Early Pompeian 156
The Fortunate Traveller 161
The Season of Phantasmal Peace 168

From

MIDSUMMER (1984)

I ("The jet bores like a silverfish through volumes of cloud")   173
II ("Companion in Rome, whom Rome makes as old as
    Rome")   174
VI ("Midsummer stretches beside me with its cat's yawn")   175
XLIX ("A wind-scraped headland, a sludgy, dishwater sea")   176
LI ("Since all of your work was really an effort to appease")   177
LIII ("There was one Syrian, with his bicycle, in our town")   178
LIV ("The midsummer sea, the hot pitch road, this grass, these
    shacks that made me")   179

From

THE ARKANSAS TESTAMENT (1987)

Saint Lucia's First Communion   183
The Light of the World   184
Night Fishing   188
Elsewhere   189
Winter Lamps   191
For Adrian   195
The Arkansas Testament   197

From

OMEROS (1990)

Chapter I (" 'This is how, one sunrise, we cut down them
    canoes' ")   213
Chapter III
    I (" *'Touchez-i, encore: N'ai fendre choux-ous-ou, salope!'* ")   219
Chapter IV
    III ("I sat on the white terrace waiting for the cheque")   221
Chapter V
    III ("How fast it fades! Maud thought; the enamelled sky")   223

Chapter XXIV ("From his heart's depth he knew she was never
        coming")   227
Chapter XXV ("Mangroves, their ankles in water, walked with
        the canoe")   233
Chapter LXIV ("I sang of quiet Achille, Afolabe's son")   239

From

THE BOUNTY (1997)

 4 Thanksgiving   247
14 ("Never get used to this; the feathery, swaying casuarinas")   248
24 ("Alphaeus Prince. What a name! He was one of the Princes")   249
26 ("The sublime always begins with the chord 'And then I saw' ")   250
27 ("Praise to the rain, eraser of picnics, praise the grey cloud") 251
31 Italian Eclogues
    I ("On the bright road to Rome, beyond Mantua")   252
34 ("At the end of this line there is an opening door")   253

From

TIEPOLO'S HOUND (2000)

    I ("They stroll on Sundays down Dronningens Street")   257
  VII
    1. ("Falling from chimneys, an exhausted arrow—")   264
    2. ("O, the exclamation of white roses, of a wet")   265
    3. ("Since light was simply particles in air")   266
 XXII ("One dawn I woke up to the gradual terror")   269
 XXIV
    3. ("I looked beyond the tarmac. A bright field")   275
    4. ("Fall; and a cool blonde crosses Christopher—")   276
XXVI ("The swallows flit in immortality")   278

From

THE PRODIGAL (2004)

2

   I ("Chasms and fissures of the vertiginous Alps")   287
   V ("On the powdery ridges of the slopes were sheds")   288

4

   IV ("I wanted to be able to write: 'There is nothing like it' ")   291

6

   III (" 'So, how was Italy?' My neighbor grinned")   293
   IV ("Blue-grey morning, sunlight shaping Jersey")   293

9

   I ("I lay on the bed near the balcony in Guadalajara")   294
   II ("I carry a small white city in my head")   294
   IV ("When we were boys coming home from the beach")   295

13

   I ("Flare of the flame tree and white egrets stalking")   298
   II ("And the first voice replied in the foam")   299
   III ("So has it come to this, to have to choose?")   300

15

   I ("*Ritorno a Milano*, if that's correct")   301

16

   II ("A grey dawn, dun. Rain-gauze shrouding the headlands")   303

17

   II ("Compare Milan, compare a glimpse of the Arno")   304

18

   III ("We were headed steadily into the open sea")   305
   IIV ("I had gaped in anticipation of an emblem")   306

INTRODUCTION

by Edward Baugh

DEREK ALTON WALCOTT was born in Castries, St. Lucia, on January 23, 1930. His parents were of modest means but appreciable social respectability, part of the island's small native bourgeoisie. St. Lucia, a tiny island in the eastern Caribbean, was then an inconsequential outpost of the British Empire.

Walcott's first published poem appeared in *The Voice of St. Lucia* on August 2, 1944, when he was fourteen years old. Titled "1944," its forty-four lines of Miltonic-Wordsworthian blank verse foreshadow the reach of his poetic ambition. Despite its derivativeness and stylistic rough edges, the poem harbors a maturity beyond the poet's years and prefigures Walcott's fiercely independent thinking—it also signals a poet who would attract controversy. In "1944," the young Walcott advanced the idea that one learns better about God from the teachings of nature than from the teachings of humankind and the Church. Three days after the poem appeared, the paper carried a rejoinder, in efficient, didactic verse, intended as an object lesson to the young poet. Its author was a Roman Catholic priest, a leader of opinion on the island, which was more than 90 percent Roman Catholic, the Walcotts being part of a minuscule Methodist minority. The priest's "Reflections" begins by patronizingly welcoming the impulse of youth to express in verse its love of nature, then proceeds to fault the young poet for his stylistic shortcomings and overreaching, as well as his lapses from tunefulness, but especially to scold him for his "wrong" teaching, which, with its "poison," threatens to undermine the authority of the Church. Questioning the role of religion and the Church, especially in St. Lucia and the West Indies, was to become a recurrent theme in Walcott's work, complicating his deep religious instinct.

Around the time that "1944" was published, Walcott had the transcendent experience, brilliantly described in Chapter 7 of *Another Life* (see page 69), that sealed his commitment to the calling of poetry and to using his poetry to "name" his island and to speak for its people. By age nineteen, he had published, at his own expense, two slim volumes, which showed a remarkably wide range of reading, including Homer, Dante, Shakespeare, Joyce, T. S. Eliot, and Pound. When he was twenty, Walcott's first major play, *Henri Christophe*, was produced in Castries by the St. Lucia Arts Guild, of which he was cofounder.

Walcott graduated from high school—St. Mary's College—in 1947, with an outstanding academic record, but having failed to win the Island Scholarship, which would have taken him to university in England and to the cosmopolitan and tradition-rich literary climate for which his intellect and imagination yearned. Instead he had to settle for teaching at his old school. Then, in 1950, he managed an escape of sorts, when, thanks to a Colonial Development and Welfare scholarship, he entered the new University College of the West Indies, at Mona, Jamaica, as one of the first students in the Faculty of Arts. (In 1973 he became the first graduate of the college to be awarded an honorary doctorate of the University of the West Indies, which the college had become.)

Though already steeped, lovingly, in English literary tradition, Walcott found the undergraduate English literature curriculum of the college hidebound, unchallenging to his own already well-informed imagination, unsatisfying to the thirst of the new Caribbean mind. This deficiency was balanced by his creative work, in poetry, drama, and painting, as well as by his being cofounder and editor of the first student magazine. These activities benefited from the stimulus of the unprecedented coming together of bright young minds from across the English-speaking Caribbean. In Jamaica, too, Walcott made two lasting and supportive literary friendships, with John Hearne, a Jamaican novelist, and John Figueroa, a Jamaican poet and professor of education.

Awarded a B.A. in 1953, Walcott remained a fourth year on the Mona campus, ostensibly reading for the diploma in education. The next three years were spent teaching on three islands, including Jamaica, where he was also a feature writer, on literature and the arts, for a weekly newspaper. In the late 1950s, he was commissioned to write *Drums and Colours*, a historical drama-chronicle, to mark the inauguration of the Federation of the West Indies. It was staged in Port of Spain, seat of the Federal Parliament, in 1958. This experience led to Walcott's falling in love with Trinidad, settling there, and founding and directing the Trinidad Theatre Workshop. Some of his most important, path-finding plays, including, most notably, *Ti-Jean and His Brothers* and *Dream on Monkey Mountain*, were written for the workshop.

In 1962, with *In a Green Night: Poems 1948–1960* (London: Jonathan Cape), Walcott enjoyed the first commercial, international publication of a collection of his poetry. Cape continued to publish his work in England until 1980, when he moved to Faber & Faber. By this time Walcott had long since broken into the United States market, as a result of the cordial professional relationship between Cape and Farrar, Straus & Giroux. The eminent American poet Robert Lowell, who had met Walcott on a visit to Trinidad and had liked the poems Walcott showed him, also recommended to his editor, Robert Giroux, that he publish Walcott, whose selected poems appeared over the Farrar, Straus imprint in 1964, and the company has been his U.S. publisher ever since.

In 1976 Walcott began to prepare himself to leave Trinidad. Shabine, the "red nigger" sailor-poet, protagonist of Walcott's popular narrative-dramatic monologue "The Schooner *Flight*," represents something of the poet's mixed feelings at the time, in loving but feeling the need to leave Trinidad. Two of Walcott's most successful plays, *Remembrance* and *Pantomime*, premiered in St. Croix, U.S. Virgin Islands (1976) and Port of Spain (1978) respectively. He soon began spending much time in the United States, doing university teaching stints. In 1982, Walcott settled at Boston University, where he still teaches creative writing on a part-time basis.

In the States, too, Walcott formed close, influential literary friendships, the most notable being with two other Farrar, Straus poets: Joseph Brodsky, the Russian exile, and Seamus Heaney, an Irishman, who would both become Nobel laureates as well. A triumvirate of top-class outsiders on the American literary scene, they shared a special admiration for the work of W. H. Auden, whom they regarded as a mentor. They collaborated on *Homage to Robert Frost* (1996), three essays in critical appreciation of the great, quintessentially American poet. Some of Walcott's best poems have been addressed to Brodsky, and when Brodsky died in 1996, Walcott was devastated.

The 1980s saw the publication of three collections of new poetry by Walcott, as well as the premieres of five new plays, including *A Branch of the Blue Nile* (1983) and *The Haitian Earth* (1984). The 1990s opened with two new works, one in poetry, the other a verse drama, which took Walcott's achievement to new heights. *Omeros* (1990) and *The Odyssey: A Stage Version*, commissioned by the Royal Shakespeare Company and premiered in 1992, brought to a high point his lifelong, sometimes uneasy engagement with Homer and the classics. The universally acclaimed *Omeros*, a kind of modern, novelized epic, is also a celebration of St. Lucia and its folk. It brought him the Nobel Prize for Literature in 1992.

More recent new plays include *Walker*, which premiered as an opera in 1993. A version of this work, based on an early, tragic episode in the African-American struggle for freedom, was published in the same volume as *The Ghost Dance* (*Walker and The Ghost Dance*), a play about a tragic episode in the history of Native American resistance to conquest and extermination by the white man.

Walcott had shown a talent for painting from childhood, and for a brief time he had hesitated between painting and poetry as his calling. Although he soon decided that the latter was his forte, he never abandoned painting: landscapes chiefly, and the occasional portrait. His painter's eye for color and light informs his poetic descriptions of landscape, and painting has been one of his themes, most sustainedly in *Another Life* (1973) and *Tiepolo's Hound* (2000). The latter, a highly selective biography of the French Impressionist painter Camille Pissarro, interfacing with the story of Walcott's own involvement with painting, is another essay in the art of the long narrative poem.

Based in St. Lucia since the mid-1990s, Walcott lives for part of the year in Greenwich Village and travels extensively across the globe to give readings, to appear at symposia on his work, and to direct his plays. From these and subsequent wanderings he returns, as in *The Prodigal* (2004), to his beloved starting place. It is supreme poetic justice that Columbus Square in Castries was renamed Derek Walcott Square after he won the Nobel Prize, the change dramatizing a country's and a region's effort, through its writers, to name and rename itself.

Walcott is perhaps the most widely acclaimed of the poets who have brought the voice of the Caribbean to the world. In his intense engagement with the local, he has asserted the importance of small places everywhere. His evocation of the sensuous experience of the Caribbean, the modulations of Caribbean light (whether benign, epiphanic, or harsh), the changes of the Caribbean Sea, generates images for apprehending Caribbean experience, for dealing with the pain of history and the colonial legacy of the region, its cultural palimpsest and mosaic. He will always figure commandingly in any consideration of the grappling with that legacy, which has been a major contribution of his generation of Anglophone Caribbean writers. His descriptive mastery of landscape, which draws on his talent as a painter, is always more than mere description, deepening into metaphor. Through his imaginative immersion in great art, he has spoken to central issues of his time, of self and society.

Speaking out of and to Caribbean experience, Walcott speaks to and for the wide world, "for such as our earth is now" ("The Season of Phantasmal Peace"), in anger at racism, at the unjust distribution of the world's wealth, at political tyranny and humankind's inhumane proclivity for violence and war. His anger is all the more eloquent because he is a poet of compassion and love and reverence for life. His representation of large and communal issues is characteristically sharpened by a subtly introduced autobiographical specificity. Running through his work is a dialogue with himself, a process of self-invention. The result is a continuously self-interrogated fictive persona in whose eyes a world takes shape.

The adventure of reading Walcott is also an adventure in poetic form and style, which one may follow chronologically through this selection. He has written excellent free verse but has been from the beginning a believer in the discipline of strict forms. Delighting in the English and classical forms that he inherited, Walcott has found his own voice in modifying, extending, and modernizing them by subtle variations and inventiveness in stanza pattern, meter, and rhyme. His achievement in this regard reached a high point in the later long narratives, beginning with *Omeros*, rigorously sustaining in each one a demanding form that is at the same time dynamically flexible and accommodating. Here also we note his modulations of voice, tone, and language, the interfusion of English and Caribbean speech, whether Anglophone or French Creole. He moves fluently from the plain and low-key to the sonorous and richly metaphorical, the courage of the large utterance.

The evolution of Walcott's craftsmanship is broadly marked by the play of two contending passions, lyric and narrative. It is perhaps only natural that the progressive extension of his poetic reach should have resulted in his recent concentration on the long narrative. But the lyric instinct is always springing in him, and he crosses forms and genres with resourcefulness and meaning-making power, incorporating lyric and dramatic modes—and even qualities of prose fiction—into narrative verse.

To move from "Prelude" to *The Prodigal* is to trace a journey that begins with a precocious setting forth, a vow of dedication to a place and a people and to the practice of poetry in their service. It is to come to a painful and self-scrutinizing awareness of what this commitment entails, including its constricting force against the instinct of imagination to go forth into the world and have access to the enlargement, and challenges, which that move may bring. It is to follow him into the fascinations and terrors of foreign landscapes and great cities, in that separation which brings a sharper knowledge of home. It is to return and return, to the benediction of one's little island but also to the realization that "there are homecomings without home" ("Homecoming: Anse la Raye"). It is to return at last as the Prodigal, to "the nurturing place of earth" (*Tiepolo's Hound*), and yet with one's eyes drawn, in the final phrase of *The Prodigal*, toward "the other shore."

This book is a distillation from the harvest of one of the great poets of the twentieth century. The difficulty was to choose, within tight limits of space, from the abundant output of over fifty years. The aim was to balance variable and overlapping criteria, by choosing poems that represent the range of Derek Walcott's work, poems that are among his best and most important, and poems that I particularly like. The pleasure of choosing was usually inseparable from the pain of having to leave out this or that particular poem.

So, if I felt a twinge of regret at having to omit "A Sea-Chantey," I rationalized that the idea and feeling it embodies are to some extent represented by "As John to Patmos" and "A City's Death by Fire." Again, I might easily have included "Oceano Nox" or "White Magic" (from *The Arkansas Testament*), but I had already chosen "Europa." I could live with omitting "North and South" (from *The Fortunate Traveller*) since "The Fortunate Traveller" remained, and the absence of "The Hotel Normandie Pool" could be compensated somewhat by the inclusion of "Early Pompeian." I also chose with an ear for how one poem speaks to or builds on another, for instance, "Ruins of a Great House" and "The Bright Field," "The Almond Trees" and "Verandah," "The Gulf" and "The Arkansas Testament."

The long narrative poems presented a particular challenge. Rather than take a little bit of this and a little bit of that from each one in order to represent all their topics and narratives, I decided for the most part and where feasible to follow one story line from each. The hope is that the chosen bits will hold together as more or less self-contained narratives that the reader may be drawn to reading through and that will stimulate him or her to read the uncut work.

From

IN A GREEN NIGHT:

POEMS 1948-1960

(1962)

I, with legs crossed along the daylight, watch
The variegated fists of clouds that gather over
The uncouth features of this, my prone island.

Meanwhile the steamers which divide horizons prove
Us lost;
Found only
In tourist booklets, behind ardent binoculars;
Found in the blue reflection of eyes
That have known cities and think us here happy.

Time creeps over the patient who are too long patient,
So I, who have made one choice,
Discover that my boyhood has gone over.

And my life, too early of course for the profound cigarette,
The turned doorhandle, the knife turning
In the bowels of the hours, must not be made public
Until I have learnt to suffer
In accurate iambics.

I go, of course, through all the isolated acts,
Make a holiday of situations,
Straighten my tie and fix important jaws,
And note the living images
Of flesh that saunter through the eye.

Until from all I turn to think how,
In the middle of the journey through my life,
O how I came upon you, my
Reluctant leopard of the slow eyes.

As John to Patmos, among the rocks and the blue, live air, hounded
His heart to peace, as here surrounded
By the strewn-silver on waves, the wood's crude hair, the rounded
Breasts of the milky bays, palms, flocks, the green and dead

Leaves, the sun's brass coin on my cheek, where
Canoes brace the sun's strength, as John, in that bleak air,
So am I welcomed richer by these blue scapes, Greek there,
So I shall voyage no more from home; may I speak here.

This island is heaven—away from the dustblown blood of cities;
See the curve of bay, watch the straggling flower, pretty is
The wing'd sound of trees, the sparse-powdered sky, when lit is
The night. For beauty has surrounded
Its black children, and freed them of homeless ditties.

As John to Patmos, in each love-leaping air,
O slave, soldier, worker under red trees sleeping, hear
What I swear now, as John did:
To praise lovelong, the living and the brown dead.

After that hot gospeller had levelled all but the churched sky,
I wrote the tale by tallow of a city's death by fire;
Under a candle's eye, that smoked in tears, I
Wanted to tell, in more than wax, of faiths that were snapped like wire.
All day I walked abroad among the rubbled tales,
Shocked at each wall that stood on the street like a liar;
Loud was the bird-rocked sky, and all the clouds were bales
Torn open by looting, and white, in spite of the fire.
By the smoking sea, where Christ walked, I asked, why
Should a man wax tears, when his wooden world fails?
In town, leaves were paper, but the hills were a flock of faiths;
To a boy who walked all day, each leaf was a green breath
Rebuilding a love I thought was dead as nails,
Blessing the death and the baptism by fire.

A wind is ruffling the tawny pelt
Of Africa. Kikuyu, quick as flies,
Batten upon the bloodstreams of the veldt.
Corpses are scattered through a paradise.
Only the worm, colonel of carrion, cries:
"Waste no compassion on these separate dead!"
Statistics justify and scholars seize
The salients of colonial policy.
What is that to the white child hacked in bed?
To savages, expendable as Jews?

Threshed out by beaters, the long rushes break
In a white dust of ibises whose cries
Have wheeled since civilization's dawn
From the parched river or beast-teeming plain.
The violence of beast on beast is read
As natural law, but upright man
Seeks his divinity by inflicting pain.
Delirious as these worried beasts, his wars
Dance to the tightened carcass of a drum,
While he calls courage still that native dread
Of the white peace contracted by the dead.

Again brutish necessity wipes its hands
Upon the napkin of a dirty cause, again
A waste of our compassion, as with Spain,
The gorilla wrestles with the superman.
I who am poisoned with the blood of both,
Where shall I turn, divided to the vein?
I who have cursed
The drunken officer of British rule, how choose
Between this Africa and the English tongue I love?
Betray them both, or give back what they give?
How can I face such slaughter and be cool?
How can I turn from Africa and live?

RUINS OF A GREAT HOUSE

though our longest sun sets at right declensions and
makes but winter arches, it cannot be long before we
lie down in darkness, and have our light in ashes . . .
                                    —BROWNE, *Urn Burial*

Stones only, the disjecta membra of this Great House,
Whose moth like girls are mixed with candledust,
Remain to file the lizard's dragonish claws.
The mouths of those gate cherubs shriek with stain;
Axle and coach wheel silted under the muck
Of cattle droppings.
                            Three crows flap for the trees
And settle, creaking the eucalyptus boughs.
A smell of dead limes quickens in the nose
The leprosy of empire.
                            "Farewell, green fields,
                            Farewell, ye happy groves!"
Marble like Greece, like Faulkner's South in stone,
Deciduous beauty prospered and is gone,
But where the lawn breaks in a rash of trees
A spade below dead leaves will ring the bone
Of some dead animal or human thing
Fallen from evil days, from evil times.

It seems that the original crops were limes
Grown in the silt that clogs the river's skirt;
The imperious rakes are gone, their bright girls gone,
The river flows, obliterating hurt.
I climbed a wall with the grille ironwork
Of exiled craftsmen protecting that great house
From guilt, perhaps, but not from the worm's rent
Nor from the padded cavalry of the mouse.
And when a wind shook in the limes I heard
What Kipling heard, the death of a great empire, the abuse
Of ignorance by Bible and by sword.

A green lawn, broken by low walls of stone,
Dipped to the rivulet, and pacing, I thought next
Of men like Hawkins, Walter Raleigh, Drake,
Ancestral murderers and poets, more perplexed
In memory now by every ulcerous crime.
The world's green age then was a rotting lime
Whose stench became the charnel galleon's text.
The rot remains with us, the men are gone.
But, as dead ash is lifted in a wind
That fans the blackening ember of the mind,
My eyes burned from the ashen prose of Donne.

Ablaze with rage I thought,
Some slave is rotting in this manorial lake,
But still the coal of my compassion fought
That Albion too was once
A colony like ours, "part of the continent, piece of the main,"
Nook-shotten, rook o'erblown, deranged
By foaming channels and the vain expense
Of bitter faction.

          All in compassion ends
So differently from what the heart arranged:
"as well as if a manor of thy friend's . . ."

Chapter I / La rivière dorée . . .

The marl white road, the Dorée rushing cool
Through gorges of green cedars, like the sound
Of infant voices from the Mission School,
Like leaves like dim seas in the mind; *ici*, Choiscul.
The stone cathedral echoes like a well,
Or as a sunken sea-cave, carved, in sand.
Touring its Via Dolorosa I tried to keep
That chill flesh from my memory when I found
A Sancta Teresa in her nest of light;
The skirts of fluttered bronze, the uplifted hand,
The cherub, shaft upraised, parting her breast.
Teach our philosophy the strength to reach
Above the navel; black bodies, wet with light,
Rolled in the spray as I strolled up the beach.

Chapter II / "Qu'un sang impur . . ."

Cosimo de Chrétien controlled a boardinghouse.
His maman managed him. No. 13.
Rue St. Louis. It had a court, with rails,
A perroquet, a curio shop where you
Saw black dolls and an old French barquentine
Anchored in glass. Upstairs, the family sword,
The rusting icon of a withered race,
Like the first angel's kept its pride of place,
Reminding the bald count to keep his word
Never to bring the lineage to disgrace.
Devouring Time, which blunts the Lion's claws,
Kept Cosimo, count of curios, fairly chaste,
For Mama's sake, for hair oil, and for whist;
Peering from balconies for his tragic twist.

9

Chapter III / *La belle qui fut . . .*

Miss Rossignol lived in the lazaretto
For Roman Catholic crones; she had white skin,
And underneath it, fine, old-fashioned bones;
She flew like bats to vespers every twilight,
The living Magdalen of Donatello;
And tipsy as a bottle when she stalked
On stilted legs to fetch the morning milk,
In a black shawl harnessed by rusty brooches.
My mother warned us how that flesh knew silk
Coursing a green estate in gilded coaches.
While Miss Rossignol, in the cathedral loft,
Sang to her one dead child, a tattered saint
Whose pride had paupered beauty to this witch
Who was so fine once, whose hands were so soft.

Chapter IV / *"Dance of Death"*

Outside I said, "He's a damned epileptic,
Your boy, El Greco! Goya, he don't lie."
Doc laughed: "Let's join the real epileptics."
Two of the girls looked good. The Indian said
That rain affects the trade. In the queer light
We all looked green. The beer and all looked green.
One draped an arm around me like a wreath.
The next talked politics. "Our mother earth,"
I said. "The great republic in whose womb
The dead outvote the quick." "Y'all too obscene,"
The Indian laughed. "Y'all college boys ain't worth
The trouble." We entered the bare room.
In the rain, walking home, was worried, but Doc said:
"Don't worry, kid, the wages of sin is birth."

The fête took place one morning in the heights
For the approval of some anthropologist.
The priests objected to such savage rites
In a Catholic country; but there was a twist
As one of the fathers was himself a student
Of black customs; it was quite ironic.
They lead sheep to the rivulet with a drum,
Dancing with absolutely natural grace
Remembered from the dark past whence we come.
The whole thing was more like a bloody picnic.
Bottles of white rum and a brawling booth.
They tie the lamb up, then chop off the head,
And ritualists take turns drinking the blood.
Great stuff, old boy; sacrifice, moments of truth.

Chapter VI

Poopa, da' was a fête! I mean it had
Free rum free whisky and some fellars beating
Pan from one of them band in Trinidad,
And everywhere you turn was people eating
And drinking and don't name me but I think
They catch his wife with two tests up the beach
While he drunk quoting Shelley with "Each
Generation has its angst, but we has none"
And wouldn't let a comma in edgewise.
(Black writer chap, one of them Oxbridge guys.)
And it was round this part once that the heart
Of a young child was torn from it alive
By two practitioners of native art,
But that was long before this jump and jive.

Chapter VII / Lotus eater . . .

"Maingot," the fisherman called that pool blocked by
Increasing filth that piled between ocean
And jungle, with a sighing grove
Of dry bamboo, its roots freckled with light
Like feathers fallen from a migratory sky.
Beyond that, the village. Through urine-stunted trees
A mud path wriggled like a snake in flight.
Franklin gripped the bridge stanchions with a hand
Trembling from fever. Each spring, memories
Of his own country where he could not die
Assaulted him. He watched the malarial light
Shiver the canes. In the tea-coloured pool, tadpoles
Seemed happy in their element. Poor, black souls.
He shook himself. Must breed, drink, rot with motion.

Chapter VIII

In the Hotel Miranda, 10 Grass St., who fought
The Falangists *en la guerra civil*, at the hour
Of bleeding light and beads of crimson dew,
This exile, with the wry face of a Jew,
Lets dust powder his pamphlets; crook't
Fingers clutch a journal to his shirt.
The eye is glacial; mountainous, the hook'd
Nose down which an ant, caballo, rides. Besides,
As pious fleas explore a seam of dirt,
The sunwashed body, past the age of sweat,
Sprawls like a hero, curiously inert.
Near him a dish of olives has turned sour.
Above the children's street cries, a girl plays
A marching song not often sung these days.

Chapter IX / "Le loupgarou"

A curious tale that threaded through the town
Through greying women sewing under eaves,
Was how his greed had brought old Le Brun down,
Greeted by slowly shutting jalousies
When he approached them in white linen suit,
Pink glasses, cork-hat, and tap-tapping cane,
A dying man licensed to sell sick fruit,
Ruined by fiends with whom he'd made a bargain.
It seems one night, these Christian witches said,
He changed himself to an Alsatian hound,
A slavering lycanthrope hot on a scent,
But his own watchman dealt the thing a wound.
It howled and lugged its entrails, trailing wet
With blood, back to its doorstep, almost dead.

Chapter X / "Adieu foulard . . ."

I watched the island narrowing the fine
Writing of foam around the precipices, then
The roads as small and casual as twine
Thrown on its mountains; I watched till the plane
Turned to the final north and turned above
The open channel with the grey sea between
The fishermen's islets until all that I love
Folded in cloud; I watched the shallow green
That broke in places where there would be reef,
The silver glinting on the fuselage, each mile
Dividing us and all fidelity strained
Till space would snap it. Then, after a while
I thought of nothing; nothing, I prayed, would change;
When we set down at Seawell it had rained.

Imprisoned in these wires of rain, I watch
This village stricken with a single street,
Each weathered shack leans on a wooden crutch,
Contented as a cripple with defeat.
Five years ago even poverty seemed sweet,
So azure and indifferent was this air,
So murmurous of oblivion the sea,
That any human action seemed a waste,
The place seemed born for being buried there.
                              The surf explodes
In scissor-birds hunting the usual fish,
The rain is muddying unpaved inland roads,
So personal grief melts in the general wish.

The hospital is quiet in the rain.
A naked boy drives pigs into the bush.
The coast shudders with every surge. The beach
Admits a beaten heron. Filth and foam.
There in a belt of emerald light, a sail
Plunges and lifts between the crests of reef,
The hills are smoking in the vaporous light,
The rain seeps slowly to the core of grief.
It could not change its sorrows and be home.

It cannot change, though you become a man
Who would exchange compassion for a drink,
Now you are brought to where manhood began
Its separation from "the wounds that make you think."
And as this rain puddles the sand, it sinks
Old sorrows in the gutter of the mind;
Where is that passionate hatred that would help
The black, the despairing, the poor, by speech alone?
The fury shakes like wet leaves in the wind,
The rain beats on a brain hardened to stone.

For there is a time in the tide of the heart, when
Arrived at its anchor of suffering, a grave
Or a bed, despairing in action, we ask,
O God, where is our home? For no one will save
The world from itself, though he walk among men,
On such shores where the foam
Murmurs oblivion of action, who raise
No cry like herons stoned by the rain.

The passionate exiles believe it, but the heart
Is circled by sorrows, by its horror
And bitter devotion to home.
The romantic nonsense ends at the bowsprit, shearing
But never arriving beyond the reef-shore foam,
Or the rain cuts us off from heaven's hearing.

Why blame the faith you have lost? Heaven remains
Where it is, in the hearts of these people,
In the womb of their church, though the rain's
Shroud is drawn across its steeple.
You are less than they are, for your truth
Consists of a general passion, a personal need,
Like that ribbed wreck, abandoned since your youth,
Washed over by the sour waves of greed.

The white rain draws its net along the coast,
A weak sun streaks the villages and beaches
And roads where laughing labourers come from shelter,
On heights where charcoal-burners heap their days.
Yet in you it still seeps, blurring each boast
Your craft has made, obscuring words and features,
Nor have you changed from all of the known ways
To leave the mind's dark cave, the most
Accursed of God's self-pitying creatures.

An old lady writes me in a spidery style,
Each character trembling, and I see a veined hand
Pellucid as paper, travelling on a skein
Of such frail thoughts its thread is often broken;
Or else the filament from which a phrase is hung
Dims to my sense, but caught, it shines like steel,
As touch a line and the whole web will feel.
She describes my father, yet I forget her face
More easily than my father's yearly dying;
Of her I remember small, buttoned boots and the place
She kept in our wooden church on those Sundays
Whenever her strength allowed;
Grey-haired, thin-voiced, perpetually bowed.

"I am Mable Rawlins," she writes, "and know both your parents";
He is dead, Miss Rawlins, but God bless your tense:
"Your father was a dutiful, honest,
Faithful, and useful person."
For such plain praise what fame is recompense?
"A horn-painter, he painted delicately on horn,
He used to sit around the table and paint pictures."
The peace of God needs nothing to adorn
It, nor glory nor ambition.
"He is twenty-eight years buried," she writes, "he was called home,
And is, I am sure, doing greater work."

The strength of one frail hand in a dim room
Somewhere in Brooklyn, patient and assured,
Restores my sacred duty to the Word.
"Home, home," she can write, with such short time to live,
Alone as she spins the blessings of her years;
Not withered of beauty if she can bring such tears,
Nor withdrawn from the world that breaks its lovers so;
Heaven is to her the place where painters go,
All who bring beauty on frail shell or horn,

There was all made, thence their *lux-mundi* drawn,
Drawn, drawn, till the thread is resilient steel,
Lost though it seems in darkening periods,
And there they return to do work that is God's.

So this old lady writes, and again I believe.
I believe it all, and for no man's death I grieve.

ISLANDS

[for Margaret]

Merely to name them is the prose
Of diarists, to make you a name
For readers who like travellers praise
Their beds and beaches as the same;
But islands can only exist
If we have loved in them. I seek,
As climate seeks its style, to write
Verse crisp as sand, clear as sunlight,
Cold as the curled wave, ordinary
As a tumbler of island water;
Yet, like a diarist, thereafter
I savour their salt-haunted rooms
(Your body stirring the creased sea
Of crumpled sheets), whose mirrors lose
Our huddled, sleeping images,
Like words which love had hoped to use
Erased with the surf's pages.

So, like a diarist in sand,
I mark the peace with which you graced
Particular islands, descending
A narrow stair to light the lamps
Against the night surf's noises, shielding
A leaping mantle with one hand,
Or simply scaling fish for supper,
Onions, jack-fish, bread, red snapper;
And on each kiss the harsh sea-taste,
And how by moonlight you were made
To study most the surf's unyielding
Patience though it seems a waste.

From

THE CASTAWAY

AND OTHER POEMS

(1 9 6 5)

The starved eye devours the seascape for the morsel
Of a sail.

The horizon threads it infinitely.

Action breeds frenzy. I lie,
Sailing the ribbed shadow of a palm,
Afraid lest my own footprints multiply.

Blowing sand, thin as smoke,
Bored, shifts its dunes.
The surf tires of its castles like a child.

The salt green vine with yellow trumpet-flower,
A net, inches across nothing.
Nothing: the rage with which the sandfly's head is filled.

Pleasures of an old man:
Morning: contemplative evacuation, considering
The dried leaf, nature's plan.

In the sun, the dog's feces
Crusts, whitens like coral.
We end in earth, from earth began.
In our own entrails, genesis.

If I listen I can hear the polyp build,
The silence thwanged by two waves of the sea.
Cracking a sea-louse, I make thunder split.

Godlike, annihilating godhead, art
And self, I abandon
Dead metaphors: the almond's leaf-like heart,

The ripe brain rotting like a yellow nut
Hatching
Its babel of sea-lice, sandfly, and maggot,

That green wine bottle's gospel choked with sand,
Labelled, a wrecked ship,
Clenched sea-wood nailed and white as a man's hand.

TARPON

At Cedros, thudding the dead sand
in spasms, the tarpon
gaped with a gold eye, drowned
thickly, thrashing with brute pain
this sea I breathe.
Stilled, its bulk,
screwed to the eye's lens, slowly
sought design. It dried like silk,
leisurely, altered to lead.
The belly, leprous, silver, bulged
like a cold chancre for the blade.
Suddenly it shuddered in immense
doubt, but the old jaw, gibbering, divulged
nothing but some new filaments
of blood. For every bloody stroke
with which a frenzied fisherman struck
its head my young son shook his head.
Could I have called out not to look
simply at the one world we shared?
Dead, and examined in detail,
a tarpon's bulk grows beautiful.

Bronze, with a brass-green mould, the scales
age like a corselet of coins,
a net of tarnished silver joins
the back's deep-sea blue to the tail's
wedged, tapering Y.
Set in a stone, triangular skull,
ringing with gold, the open eye
is simply, tiringly there.
A shape so simple, like a cross,
a child could draw it in the air.
A tarpon's scale, its skin's flake
washed at the sea's edge and held
against the light, looks just like what

the grinning fisherman said it would:
dense as frost glass but delicate,
etched by a diamond, it showed
a child's drawing of a ship,
the sails' twin triangles, a mast.

Can such complexity of shape,
such bulk, terror, and fury fit
in a design so innocent,
that through opaque, phantasmal mist,
moving, but motionlessly, it
sails where imagination sent?

THE FLOCK

The grip of winter tightening, its thinned
volleys of blue-wing teal and mallard fly
from the longbows of reeds bent by the wind,
arrows of yearning for our different sky.
A season's revolution hones their sense,
whose target is our tropic light, while I
awoke this sunrise to a violence
of images migrating from the mind.
Skeletal forest, a sepulchral knight
riding in silence at a black tarn's edge,
hooves cannonading snow
in the white funeral of the year,
ant-like across the forehead of an alp
in iron contradiction crouched
against those gusts that urge the mallards south.
Vizor'd with blind defiance of his quest,
its yearly divination of the spring.
I travel through such silence, making dark
symbols with this pen's print across snow,
measuring winter's augury by words
settling the branched mind like migrating birds,
and never question when they come or go.

The style, tension of motion and the dark,
inflexible direction of the world
as it revolves upon its centuries
with change of language, climate, customs, light,
with our own prepossession day by day
year after year with images of flight,
survive our condemnation and the sun's
exultant larks.
                    The dark impartial Arctic,
whose glaciers encased the mastodon,
froze giant minds in marble attitudes,
revolves with tireless, determined grace

upon an iron axle, though the seals
howl with inhuman cries across its ice
and pages of torn birds are blown across
whitening tundras like engulfing snow.

Till its annihilation may the mind
reflect his fixity through winter, tropic,
until that equinox when the clear eye
clouds, like a mirror, without contradiction,
greet the black wings that cross it as a blessing
like the high, whirring flock that flew across
the cold sky of this page when I began
this journey by the wintry flare of dawn,
flying by instinct to their secret places,
both for their need and for my sense of season.

LAVENTILLE

[*for V. S. Naipaul*]

To find the Western Path
Through the Gates of Wrath—
                        —BLAKE

It huddled there
steel tinkling its blue painted metal air,
tempered in violence, like Rio's favelas,

with snaking, perilous streets whose edges fell as
its Episcopal turkey-buzzards fall
from its miraculous hilltop

shrine,
down the impossible drop
to Belmont, Woodbrook, Maraval, St. Clair

that shine
like peddlers' tin trinkets in the sun.
From a harsh

shower, its gutters growled and gargled wash
past the Youth Centre, past the water catchment,
a rigid children's carousel of cement;

we climbed where lank electric
lines and tension cables linked its raw brick
hovels like a complex feud,

where the inheritors of the middle passage stewed,
five to a room, still clamped below their hatch,
breeding like felonies,

whose lives revolve round prison, graveyard, church.
Below bent breadfruit trees
in the flat, coloured city, class

escalated into structures still,
merchant, middleman, magistrate, knight. To go downhill
from here was to ascend.

The middle passage never guessed its end.
This is the height of poverty
for the desperate and black;

climbing, we could look back
with widening memory
on the hot, corrugated-iron sea
whose horrors we all

shared. The salt blood knew it well,
you, me, Samuel's daughter, Samuel,
and those ancestors clamped below its grate.

And climbing steeply past the wild
gutters, it shrilled
in the blood, for those who suffered, who were killed,

and who survive.
What other gift was there to give
as the godparents of his unnamed child?

Yet outside the brown annex of the church, the
stifling odour of bay rum and talc, the particular,
neat sweetness of the crowd distressed

that sense. The black, fawning verger,
his bow tie akimbo, grinning, the clown-gloved
fashionable wear of those I deeply loved

once, made me look on with hopelessness and rage
at their new, apish habits, their excess
and fear, the possessed, the self-possessed;

their perfume shrivelled to a childhood fear
of Sabbath graveyards, christenings, marriages,
that muggy, steaming, self-assuring air

of tropical Sabbath afternoons. And in
the church, eyes prickling with rage,
the children rescued from original sin

by their Godfather since the middle passage,
the supercilious brown curate, who intones,
healing the guilt in these rachitic bones,
twisting my love within me like a knife:
"across the troubled waters of this life . . ."

Which of us cares to walk
even if God wished
those retching waters where our souls were fished

for this new world? Afterwards, we talk
in whispers, close to death
among these stones planted on alien earth.

Afterwards,
the ceremony, the careful photograph
moved out of range before the patient tombs,

we dare a laugh,
ritual, desperate words,
born like these children from habitual wombs,

from lives fixed in the unalterable groove
of grinding poverty. I stand out on a balcony
and watch the sun pave its flat, golden path

across the roofs, the aerials, cranes, the tops
of fruit trees crawling downward to the city.
Something inside is laid wide like a wound,

some open passage that has cleft the brain,
some deep, amnesiac blow. We left
somewhere a life we never found,

customs and gods that are not born again,
some crib, some grille of light
clanged shut on us in bondage, and withheld

us from that world below us and beyond,
and in its swaddling cerements we're still bound.

THE ALMOND TREES

There's nothing here
this early;
cold sand
cold churning ocean, the Atlantic,
no visible history,

except this stand
of twisted, coppery, sea-almond trees
their shining postures surely
bent as metal, and one

foam-haired, salt-grizzled fisherman,
his mongrel growling, whirling on the stick
he pitches him; its spinning rays
"no visible history"
until their lengthened shapes amaze the sun.

By noon,
this further shore of Africa is strewn
with the forked limbs of girls toasting their flesh
in scarves, sunglasses, Pompeian bikinis,
brown daphnes, laurels, they'll all have
like their originals, their sacred grove:
this frieze
of twisted, coppery, sea-almond trees.

The fierce acetylene air
has singed
their writhing trunks with rust, the same
hues as a foundered, peeling barge.
It'll sear a pale skin copper with its flame.

The sand's white-hot ash underheel,
but their aged limbs have got their brazen sheen
from fire. Their bodies fiercely shine!

They're cured,
they endured their furnace.

Aged trees and oiled limbs share a common colour!

Welded in one flame,
huddling naked, stripped of their name,
for Greek or Roman tags, they were lashed
raw by wind, washed
out with salt and fire-dried,
bitterly nourished where their branches died,

their leaves' broad dialect a coarse,
enduring sound
they shared together.

Not as some running hamadryad's cries
rooted, broke slowly into leaf
her nipples peaking to smooth, wooden boles

their grief
howls seaward through charred, ravaged holes.

One sunburnt body now acknowledges
that past and its own metamorphosis
as, moving from the sun, she kneels to spread
her wrap within the bent arms of this grove
that grieves in silence, like parental love.

VERANDAH

[*for Ronald Bryden*]

Grey apparitions at verandah ends
like smoke, divisible, but one
your age is ashes, its coherence gone,

Planters whose tears were marketable gum, whose voices
scratch the twilight like dried fronds
edged with reflection,

Colonels, hard as the commonwealth's greenheart,
middlemen, usurers whose art
kept an empire in the red,

Upholders of Victoria's china seas
lapping embossed around a drinking mug,
bully-boy roarers of the empire club,

To the tarantara of the bugler, the sunset furled
round the last post,
the "flamingo colours" of a fading world,

A ghost steps from you, my grandfather's ghost!
Uprooted from some rainy English shire,
you sought your Roman

End in suicide by fire.
Your mixed son gathered your charred blackened bones
in a child's coffin.

And buried them himself on a strange coast.
Sire,
why do I raise you up? Because

Your house has voices, your burnt house
shrills with unguessed, lovely inheritors,
your genealogical roof tree, fallen, survives,
like seasoned timber through green, little lives.

I ripen towards your twilight, sir, that dream
where I am singed in that sea-crossing, steam
towards that vaporous world, whose souls,

Like pressured trees, brought diamonds out of coals.
The sparks pitched from your burning house are stars.
I am the man my father loved and was.

I climb the stair
and stretch a darkening hand to greet those friends
who share with you the last inheritance
of earth, our shrine and pardoner,

grey, ghostly loungers at verandah ends.

CRUSOE'S ISLAND

I

The chapel's cowbell
Like God's anvil
Hammers ocean to a blinding shield;
Fired, the sea grapes slowly yield
Bronze plates to the metallic heat.

Red, corrugated-iron
Roofs roar in the sun.
The wiry, ribbed air
Above earth's open kiln
Writhes like a child's vision
Of hell, but nearer, nearer.

Below, the picnic plaid
Of Scarborough is spread
To a blue, perfect sky,
Dome of our hedonist philosophy.
Bethel and Canaan's heart
Lies open like a psalm.
I labour at my art.
My father, God, is dead.

Past thirty now I know
To love the self is dread
Of being swallowed by the blue
Of heaven overhead
Or rougher blue below.
Some lesion of the brain
From art or alcohol
Flashes this fear by day:
As startling as his shadow
Grows to the castaway.

Upon this rock the bearded hermit built
His Eden:
Goats, corn crop, fort, parasol, garden,
Bible for Sabbath, all the joys
But one
Which sent him howling for a human voice.
Exiled by a flaming sun
The rotting nut, bowled in the surf,
Became his own brain rotting from the guilt
Of heaven without his kind,
Crazed by such paradisal calm
The spinal shadow of a palm
Built keel and gunwale in his mind.

The second Adam since the fall,
His germinal
Corruption held the seed
Of that congenital heresy that men fail
According to their creed.
Craftsman and castaway,
All heaven in his head,
He watched his shadow pray
Not for God's love but human love instead.

II

We came here for the cure
Of quiet in the whelk's centre,
From the fierce, sudden quarrel,
From kitchens where the mind,
Like bread, disintegrates in water,
To let a salt sun scour
The brain as harsh as coral,
To bathe like stones in wind,
To be, like beast or natural object, pure.

That fabled, occupational
Compassion, supposedly inherited with the gift
Of poetry, had fed
With a rat's thrift on faith, shifted
Its trust to corners, hoarded
Its mania like bread,
Its brain a white, nocturnal bloom
That in a drunken, moonlit room
Saw my son's head
Swaddled in sheets
Like a lopped nut, lolling in foam.

O love, we die alone!
I am borne by the bell
Backward to boyhood
To the grey wood
Spire, harvest and marigold,
To those whom a cruel
Just God could gather
To His blue breast, His beard
A folding cloud,
As He gathered my father.
Irresolute and proud,
I can never go back.

I have lost sight of hell,
Of heaven, of human will,
My skill
Is not enough,
I am struck by this bell
To the root.
Crazed by a racking sun,
I stand at my life's noon,
On parched, delirious sand
My shadow lengthens.

III

Art is profane and pagan,
The most it has revealed
Is what a crippled Vulcan
Beat on Achilles' shield.
By these blue, changing graves
Fanned by the furnace blast
Of heaven, may the mind
Catch fire till it cleaves
Its mould of clay at last.

Now Friday's progeny,
The brood of Crusoe's slave,
Black little girls in pink
Organdy, crinolines,
Walk in their air of glory
Beside a breaking wave;
Below their feet the surf
Hisses like tambourines.

At dusk, when they return
For vespers, every dress
Touched by the sun will burn
A seraph's, an angel's,
And nothing I can learn
From art or loneliness
Can bless them as the bell's
Transfiguring tongue can bless.

CODICIL

Schizophrenic, wrenched by two styles,
one a hack's hired prose, I earn
my exile. I trudge this sickle, moonlit beach for miles,

tan, burn
to slough off
this love of ocean that's self-love.

To change your language you must change your life.

I cannot right old wrongs.
Waves tire of horizon and return.
Gulls screech with rusty tongues

Above the beached, rotting pirogues,
they were a venomous beaked cloud at Charlotteville.

Once I thought love of country was enough,
now, even if I chose, there's no room at the trough.

I watch the best minds root like dogs
for scraps of favour.
I am nearing middle

age, burnt skin
peels from my hand like paper, onion-thin,
like Peer Gynt's riddle.

At heart there's nothing, not the dread
of death. I know too many dead.
They're all familiar, all in character,

even how they died. On fire,
the flesh no longer fears that furnace mouth
of earth,

that kiln or ashpit of the sun,
nor this clouding, unclouding sickle moon
whitening this beach again like a blank page.

All its indifference is a different rage.

From

THE GULF

AND OTHER POEMS

(1 9 6 9)

MASS MAN

Through a great lion's head clouded by mange
a black clerk growls.
Next, a gold-wired peacock withholds a man,
a fan, flaunting its oval, jewelled eyes;
What metaphors!
What coruscating, mincing fantasies!

Hector Mannix, waterworks clerk, San Juan, has entered a lion,
Boysie, two golden mangoes bobbing for breastplates, barges
like Cleopatra down her river, making style.
"Join us," they shout. "Oh God, child, you can't dance?"
But somewhere in that whirlwind's radiance
a child, rigged like a bat, collapses, sobbing.

But I am dancing, look, from an old gibbet
my bull-whipped body swings, a metronome!
Like a fruit bat dropped in the silk-cotton's shade,
my mania, my mania is a terrible calm.

Upon your penitential morning,
some skull must rub its memory with ashes,
some mind must squat down howling in your dust,
some hand must crawl and recollect your rubbish,
someone must write your poems.

HOMAGE TO EDWARD THOMAS

Formal, informal, by a country's cast
topography delineates its verse,
erects the classic bulk, for rigid contrast
of sonnet, rectory or this manor house
dourly timbered against these sinuous
Downs, defines the formal and informal prose
of Edward Thomas's poems, which make this garden
return its subtle scent of Edward Thomas
in everything here hedged or loosely grown.
Lines which you once dismissed as tenuous
because they would not howl or overwhelm,
as crookedly grave-bent, or cuckoo-dreaming,
seeming dissoluble as this Sussex down
harden in their indifference, like this elm.

THE GULF

[for Jack and Barbara Harrison]

I

The airport coffee tastes less of America.
Sour, unshaven, dreading the exertion
of tightening, racked nerves fuelled with liquor,

some smoky, resinous bourbon,
the body, buckling at its casket hole,
a roar like last night's blast racing its engines,

watches the fumes of the exhausted soul
as the trans-Texas jet, screeching, begins
its flight and friends diminish. So, to be aware

of the divine union the soul detaches
itself from created things. "We're in the air,"
the Texan near me grins. All things: these matches

from LBJ's campaign hotel, this rose
given me at dawn in Austin by a child,
this book of fables by Borges, its prose

a stalking, moonlit tiger. What was willed
on innocent, sun-streaked Dallas, the beast's claw
curled round that hairspring rifle is revealed

on every page as lunacy or feral law;
circling that wound we leave Love Field.
Fondled, these objects conjure hotels,

quarrels, new friendships, brown limbs
nakedly moulded as these autumn hills
memory penetrates as the jet climbs

the new clouds over Texas; their home means
an island suburb, forest, mountain water;
they are the simple properties for scenes

whose joy exhausts like grief, scenes where we learn,
exchanging the least gifts, this rose, this napkin,
that those we love are objects we return,

that this lens on the desert's wrinkled skin
has priced our flesh, all that we love in pawn
to that brass ball, that the gifts, multiplying,

clutter and choke the heart, and that I shall
watch love reclaim its things as I lie dying.
My very flesh and blood! Each seems a petal

shrivelling from its core. I watch them burn,
by the nerves' flare I catch their skeletal
candour! Best never to be born,

the great dead cry. Their works shine on our shelves,
by twilight tour their gilded gravestone spines,
and read until the lamplit page revolves

to a white stasis whose detachment shines
like a propeller's rainbowed radiance.
Circling like us; no comfort for their loves!

II

The cold glass darkens. Elizabeth wrote once
that we make glass the image of our pain;
I watch clouds boil past the cold, sweating pane

above the Gulf. All styles yearn to be plain
as life. The face of the loved object under glass
is plainer still. Yet, somehow, at this height,

46

above this cauldron boiling with its wars,
our old earth, breaking to familiar light,
that cloud-bound mummy with self-healing scars

peeled of her cerements again looks new;
some cratered valley heals itself with sage,
through that grey, fading massacre a blue

lighthearted creek flutes of some siege
to the amnesia of drumming water.
Their cause is crystalline: the divine union

of these detached, divided states, whose slaughter
darkens each summer now, as one by one,
the smoke of bursting ghettos clouds the glass

down every coast where filling station signs
proclaim the Gulf, an air, heavy with gas,
sickens the state, from Newark to New Orleans.

III

Yet the South felt like home. Wrought balconies,
the sluggish river with its tidal drawl,
the tropic air charged with the extremities

of patience, a heat heavy with oil,
canebrakes, that legendary jazz. But fear
thickened my voice, that strange, familiar soil

prickled and barbed the texture of my hair,
my status as a secondary soul.
The Gulf, your gulf, is daily widening.

each blood-red rose warns of that coming night
when there's no rock cleft to go hidin' in
and all the rocks catch fire, when that black might,

their stalking, moonless panthers turn from Him
whose voice they can no more believe, when the black X's
mark their passover with slain seraphim.

IV

The Gulf shines, dull as lead. The coast of Texas
glints like a metal rim. I have no home
as long as summer bubbling to its head

boils for that day when in the Lord God's name
the coals of fire are heaped upon the head
of all whose gospel is the whip and flame,

age after age, the uninstructing dead.

BLUES

Those five or six young guys
hunched on the stoop
that oven-hot summer night
whistled me over. Nice
and friendly. So, I stop.
MacDougal or Christopher
Street in chains of light.

A summer festival. Or some
saint's. I wasn't too far from
home, but not too bright
for a nigger, and not too dark.
I figured we were all
one, wop, nigger, jew,
besides, this wasn't Central Park.
I'm coming on too strong? You figure
right! They beat this yellow nigger
black and blue.

Yeah. During all this, scared
in case one used a knife,
I hung my olive-green, just-bought
sports coat on a fire plug.
I did nothing. They fought
each other, really. Life
gives them a few kicks,
that's all. The spades, the spicks.

My face smashed in, my bloody mug
pouring, my olive-branch jacket saved
from cuts and tears,
I crawled four flights upstairs.
Sprawled in the gutter, I
remember a few watchers waved
loudly, and one kid's mother shouting

like "Jackie" or "Terry,"
"now that's enough!"
It's nothing really.
They don't get enough love.

You know they wouldn't kill
you. Just playing rough,
like young America will.
Still, it taught me something
about love. If it's so tough,
forget it.

AIR

*There has been romance, but it has been the romance of
pirates and outlaws. The natural graces of life do not
show themselves under such conditions. There are no
people there in the true sense of the word, with a
character and purpose of their own.*

         —FROUDE, *The Bow of Ulysses*

The unheard, omnivorous
jaws of this rain forest
not merely devour all
but allow nothing vain;
they never rest,
grinding their disavowal
of human pain.

Long, long before us,
those hot jaws, like an oven
steaming, were open
to genocide; they devoured
two minor yellow races, and
half of a black;
in the Word made flesh of God
all entered that gross un-
discriminating stomach;

the forest is unconverted,
because that shell-like noise
which roars like silence, or
ocean's surpliced choirs
entering its nave, to a censer
of swung mist, is not
the rustling of prayer
but nothing; milling air,
a faith, infested, cannibal,
which eats gods, which devoured

the god-refusing Carib, petal
by golden petal, then forgot,
and the Arawak
who leaves not the lightest fern-trace
of his fossil to be cultured
by black rock,

but only the rusting cries
of a rainbird, like a hoarse
warrior summoning his race
from vaporous air
between this mountain ridge
and the vague sea
where the lost exodus
of corials sunk without trace—

there is too much nothing here.

LANDFALL, GRENADA

[*for Robert Head, mariner*]

Where you are rigidly anchored,
the groundswell of blue foothills, the blown canes
surging to cumuli cannot be heard;
like the slow, seamless ocean,
one motion folds the grass where you were lowered,
and the tiered sea
whose grandeurs you detested
climbs out of sound.

Its moods held no mythology
for you, it was a working place
of tonnage and ruled stars;
you chose your landfall with a mariner's
casual certainty,
calm as that race
into whose heart you harboured;
your death was a log's entry,
your suffering held the strenuous
reticence of those
whose rites are never public,
hating to impose, to offend.
Deep friend, teach me to learn
such ease, such landfall going,
such mocking tolerance of those
neat gravestone elegies
that rhyme our end.

HOMECOMING: ANSE LA RAYE

[*for Garth St. Omer*]

Whatever else we learned
at school, like solemn Afro-Greeks eager for grades,
of Helen and the shades
of borrowed ancestors,
there are no rites
for those who have returned,
only, when her looms fade,
drilled in our skulls, the doom-
surge-haunted nights,
only this well-known passage

under the coconuts' salt-rusted
swords, these rotted
leathery sea-grape leaves,
the seacrabs' brittle helmets, and
this barbecue of branches, like the ribs
of sacrificial oxen on scorched sand;
only this fish-gut-reeking beach
whose frigates tack like buzzards overhead,
whose spindly, sugar-headed children race
pelting up from the shallows
because your clothes,
your posture
seem a tourist's.
They swarm like flies
round your heart's sore.

Suffer them to come,
entering your needle's eye,
knowing whether they live or die,
what others make of life will pass them by
like that far silvery freighter
threading the horizon like a toy;

for once, like them,
you wanted no career
but this sheer light, this clear,
infinite, boring, paradisal sea,
but hoped it would mean something to declare
today, I am your poet, yours,
all this you knew,
but never guessed you'd come
to know there are homecomings without home.

You give them nothing.
Their curses melt in air.
The black cliffs scowl,
the ocean sucks its teeth,
like that dugout canoe
a drifting petal fallen in a cup,
with nothing but its image,
you sway, reflecting nothing.
The freighter's silvery ghost
is gone, the children gone.
Dazed by the sun
you trudge back to the village
past the white, salty esplanade
under whose palms dead
fishermen move their draughts in shade,
crossing, eating their islands,
and one, with a politician's
ignorant, sweet smile, nods,
as if all fate
swayed in his lifted hand.

NEARING FORTY

[*for John Figueroa*]

Insomniac since four, hearing this narrow,
rigidly metred, early-rising rain
recounting, as its coolness numbs the marrow,
that I am nearing forty, nearer the weak
vision thickening to a frosted pane,
nearer the day when I may judge my work
by the bleak modesty of middle age
as a false dawn, fireless and average,
which would be just, because your life bled for
the household truth, the style past metaphor
that finds its parallel however wretched
in simple, shining lines, in pages stretched
plain as a bleaching bedsheet under a gutter-
ing rainspout, glad for the sputter
of occasional insight; you who foresaw
ambition as a searing meteor
will fumble a damp match and, smiling, settle
for the dry wheezing of a dented kettle,
for vision narrower than a louvre's gap,
then, watching your leaves thin, recall how deep
prodigious cynicism plants its seed,
gauges our seasons by this year's end rain
which, as greenhorns at school, we'd
call conventional for convectional;
or you will rise and set your lines to work
with sadder joy but steadier elation,

until the night when you can really sleep,
measuring how imagination
ebbs, conventional as any water clerk
who weighs the force of lightly falling rain,
which, as the new moon moves it, does its work
even when it seems to weep.

From

ANOTHER LIFE

(1 9 7 3)

CHAPTER 1

I

Verandahs, where the pages of the sea
are a book left open by an absent master
in the middle of another life—
I begin here again,
begin until this ocean's
a shut book, and like a bulb
the white moon's filaments wane.

Begin with twilight, when a glare
which held a cry of bugles lowered
the coconut lances of the inlet,
as a sun, tired of empire, declined.
It mesmerized like fire without wind,
and as its amber climbed
the beer-stein ovals of the British fort
above the promontory, the sky
grew drunk with light.
                        There
was your heaven! The clear
glaze of another life,
a landscape locked in amber, the rare
gleam. The dream
of reason had produced its monster:
a prodigy of the wrong age and colour.

All afternoon the student
with the dry fever of some draughtsman's clerk
had magnified the harbour, now twilight
eager to complete itself,
drew a girl's figure to the open door
of a stone boathouse with a single stroke, then fell
to a reflecting silence. This silence waited
for the verification of detail:

the gables of the St. Antoine Hotel
aspiring from jungle, the flag
at Government House melting its pole,
and for the tidal amber glare to glaze
the last shacks of the Morne till they became
transfigured sheerly by the student's will,
a cinquecento fragment in gilt frame.

The vision died,
the black hills simplified
to hunks of coal,
but if the light was dying through the stone
of that converted boathouse on the pier,
a girl, blowing its embers in her kitchen,
could feel its epoch entering her hair.

Darkness, soft as amnesia, furred the slope.
He rose and climbed towards the studio.
The last hill burned,
the sea crinkled like foil,
a moon ballooned up from the Wireless Station. O
mirror, where a generation yearned
for whiteness, for candour, unreturned.

The moon maintained her station,
her fingers stroked a chiton-fluted sea,
her disc whitewashed the shells
of gutted offices barnacling the wharves
of the burnt town, her lamp
baring the ovals of toothless façades,
along the Roman arches, as he passed
her alternating ivories lay untuned,
her age was dead, her sheet
shrouded the antique furniture, the mantel
with its plaster-of-Paris Venus, which
his yearning had made marble, half-cracked
unsilvering mirror of black servants,
like the painter's kerchiefed, ear-ringed portrait: Albertina.

Within the door, a bulb
haloed the tonsure of a reader crouched
in its pale tissue like an embryo,
the leisured gaze
turned towards him, the short arms
yawned briefly, welcome. Let us see.
Brown, balding, a lacertilian
jut to its underlip,
with spectacles thick as a glass paperweight
over eyes the hue of sea-smoothed bottle glass,
the man wafted the drawing to his face
as if dusk were myopic, not his gaze.
Then, with slow strokes, the master changed the sketch.

II

In its dimension the drawing could not trace
the sociological contours of the promontory;
once, it had been an avenue of palms
strict as Hobbema's aisle of lowland poplars,
now, levelled, bulldozed, and metalled for an airstrip,
its terraces like tree rings told its age.
There, patriarchal banyans,
bearded with vines from which black schoolboys gibboned,
brooded on a lagoon seasoned with dead leaves,
mangroves knee-deep in water
crouched like whelk pickers on brown, spindly legs
scattering red soldier crabs
scrabbling for redcoats' meat.
The groves were sawn
symmetry and contour crumbled,
down the arched barrack balconies
where colonels in the whisky-coloured light
had watched the green flash, like a lizard's tongue,
catch the last sail, tonight
row after row of orange stamps repeated
the villas of promoted civil servants.

The moon came to the window and stayed there.
He was her subject, changing when she changed,
from childhood he'd considered palms
ignobler than imagined elms,
the breadfruit's splayed
leaf coarser than the oak's,
he had prayed
nightly for his flesh to change,
his dun flesh peeled white by her lightning strokes!
Above the cemetery where
the airstrip's tarmac ended
her slow disc magnified
the life beneath her like a reading glass.

Below the bulb
a green book, laid
face downward. Moon,
and sea. He read
the spine. FIRST POEMS:
CAMPBELL. The painter
almost absently
reversed it, and began to read:

> "Holy be
> the white head of a Negro,
> sacred be
> the black flax of a black child . . ."

And from a new book,
bound in sea-green linen, whose lines
matched the exhilaration which their reader,
rowing the air around him now, conveyed,
another life it seemed would start again,
while past the droning, tonsured head
the white face
of a dead child stared from its window frame.

CHAPTER 2

        Maman,
only on Sundays was the Singer silent,
then
tobacco smelt stronger, was more masculine.
Sundays
the parlour smelt of uncles,
the lamp poles rang,
the drizzle shivered its maracas,
like mandolins the tightening wires of rain,
then
from striped picnic buses, *jour marron,*
gold bangles tinkled like good-morning in Guinea
and a whore's laughter opened like sliced fruit.

Maman,
you sat folded in silence,
as if your husband might walk up the street,
while in the forests the cicadas pedalled their machines,
and silence, a black maid in white,
barefooted, polished and repolished
the glass across his fading watercolours,
the dumb Victrola cabinet,
the panels and the gleam of blue-winged teal
beating the mirror's lake.
In silence,
the revered, silent objects ring like glass,
at my eyes' touch, everything tightened, tuned,
Sunday,
the dead Victrola;

Sunday, a child
breathing with lungs of bread;
Sunday, the sacred silence of machines.

Maman,
your son's ghost circles your lost house, looking in
incomprehensibly at its dumb tenants
like fishes busily inaudible behind glass,
while the carpenter's Gothic joke, A, W, A, W,
Warwick and Alix involved in its eaves
breaks with betrayal.
You stitched us clothes from the nearest elements,
made shirts of rain and freshly ironed clouds,
then, singing your iron hymn, you riveted
your feet on Monday to the old machine.

                                               *

Then Monday plunged her arms up to the elbows
in a foam tub, under a blue-soap sky,
the wet fleets sailed the yard, and every bubble,
with its bent, mullioned window, opened
its mote of envy in the child's green eye
of that sovereign-headed, pink-cheeked bastard Bubbles
in the frontispiece of *Pears Cyclopedia*.
Rising in crystal spheres, world after world.

They melt from you, your sons.
Your arms grow full of rain.

    III

Old house, old woman, old room,
old planes, old buckling membranes of the womb,
translucent walls,
breathe through your timbers; gasp
arthritic, curling beams,
cough in old air
shining with motes, stair
polished and repolished by the hands of strangers,
die with defiance flecking your grey eyes,
motes of a sunlit air,
your timbers humming with constellations of carcinoma,

your bed frames glowing with radium,
cold iron dilating the fever of your body,
while the galvanized iron snaps in spasms of pain,
but a house gives no outcry,
it bears the depth of forest, of ocean and mother.
Each consuming the other
with memory and unuse.

Why should we weep for dumb things?

This radiance of sharing extends to the simplest objects,
to a favourite hammer, a paintbrush, a toothless,
gum-sunken old shoe,
to the brain of a childhood room, retarded,
lobotomized of its furniture,
stuttering its inventory of accidents:
why this chair cracked,
when did the tightened scream
of that bedspring finally snap,
when did that unsilvering mirror finally
surrender her vanity,
and, in turn, these objects assess us,
that yellow paper flower with the eyes of a cat,
that stain, familiar as warts or some birthmark,
as the badge of some loved defect,

while the thorns of the bougainvillea
moult like old fingernails,
and the flowers keep falling,
and the flowers keep opening,
the allamandas' fallen bugles, but nobody charges.

Skin wrinkles like paint,
the forearm of a balustrade freckles,
crows' feet radiate
from the shut eyes of windows,
and the door, mouth clamped, reveals nothing,
for there is no secret,

there is no other secret
but a pain so alive that
to touch every ledge of that house edges a scream
from the burning wires, the nerves
with their constellation of cancer,
the beams with their star-seed of lice,
pain shrinking every room,
pain shining in every womb,
while the blind, dumb
termites, with jaws of the crabcells consume,
in silent thunder,
to the last of all Sundays,
consume.

Finger each object, lift it
from its place, and it screams again
to be put down
in its ring of dust, like the marriage finger
frantic without its ring;
I can no more move you from your true alignment,
Mother, than we can move objects in paintings.

Your house sang softly of balance,
of the rightness of placed things.

CHAPTER 7

II

About the August of my fourteenth year
I lost my self somewhere above a valley
owned by a spinster-farmer, my dead father's friend.
At the hill's edge there was a scarp
with bushes and boulders stuck in its side.
Afternoon light ripened the valley,
rifling smoke climbed from small labourers' houses,
and I dissolved into a trance.
I was seized by a pity more profound
than my young body could bear, I climbed
with the labouring smoke,
I drowned in labouring breakers of bright cloud,
then uncontrollably I began to weep,
inwardly, without tears, with a serene extinction
of all sense; I felt compelled to kneel,
I wept for nothing and for everything,
I wept for the earth of the hill under my knees,
for the grass, the pebbles, for the cooking smoke
above the labourers' houses like a cry,
for unheard avalanches of white cloud,
but "darker grows the valley, more and more forgetting."
For their lights still shine through the hovels like litmus,
the smoking lamp still slowly says its prayer,
the poor still move behind their tinted scrim,
the taste of water is still shared everywhere,
but in that ship of night, locked in together,
through which, like chains, a little light might leak,
something still fastens us forever to the poor.

But which was the true light?
Blare noon or twilight,
"the lonely light that Samuel Palmer engraved,"
or the cold

iron entering the soul, as the soul sank
out of belief.
              That bugle-coloured twilight
blew the withdrawal not of legions and proconsuls,
but of pale, prebendary clerks, with the gait and gall
of camels. And yet I envied them,
bent, silent decipherers of sacred texts,
their Roman arches, Virgilian terraces,
their tiered, ordered colonial world
where evening, like the talons of a bird
bent the blue jacaranda softly, and smoke rose with
the leisure and frailty of recollection,
I learnt their strict necrology of dead kings,
bones freckling the rushes of damp tombs,
the light-furred luminous world of Claude,
their ruined temples, and in drizzling twilights, Turner.

III

Our father,
              who floated in the vaults of Michelangelo,
St. Raphael,
              of sienna and gold leaf,
it was then
              that he fell in love, having no care
for truth,
              that he could enter the doorway of a triptych,
that he believed
              those three stiff horsemen cantering past a rock,
              towards jewelled cities on a cracked horizon,
              that the lances of Uccello shivered him,
              like Saul, unhorsed,
that he fell in love with art,
              and life began.

IV

Noon,
          and its sacred water sprinkles.
A schoolgirl in blue and white uniform,
her golden plaits a simple coronet
out of Angelico, a fine sweat on her forehead,
hair where the twilight singed and signed its epoch.
And a young man going home.
They move away from each other.
They are moving towards each other.
His head roars with hunger and poems.
His hand is trembling to recite her name.
She clutches her books, she is laughing,
her uniformed companions laughing.
She laughs till she is near tears.

V

Who could tell, in "the crossing of that pair"
          that later it would mean
that rigid iron lines were drawn between
          him and that garden chair
from which she rose to greet him, as for a train,
          that watching her rise
from the bright boathouse door was like some station
          where either stood, transfixed
by the rattling telegraph of carriage windows
          flashing goodbyes,
that every dusk rehearsed a separation
          already in their eyes,
that later, when they sat in silence, seaward,
          and, looking upward, heard
its engines as some moonlit liner chirred
          from the black harbour outward,
those lights spelt out their sentence, word by word?

CHAPTER 9

I

There are already, invisible on canvas,
lines locking into outlines. The visible dissolves
in a benign acid. The leaf
insists on its oval echo, that wall
breaks into sweat, oil settles
in the twin pans of the eyes.

Blue, on the tip of the tongue,
and this cloud can go no further.
Over your shoulder the landscape
frowns at its image. A rigour
of zinc white seizes the wall,
April ignites the immortelle,
the leaf of a kneeling sapling
is the yellow flame of Lippi's *Annunciation*.
Like the scrape of a struck match, cadmium orange,
evened to the wick of a lantern.
Like a crowd, surrounding the frame,
the muttering variegations of green.

The mountain's crouching back begins to ache.

The eyes sweat, small fires gnaw
at the edge of the canvas,
ochre, sienna, their smoke
billows into blue cloud.
A bird's cry tries to pierce
the thick silence of canvas.
From the reeds of your lashes, the wild commas
of crows are beginning to rise.
At your feet
the dead cricket grows into a dragon,
the razor grass bristles resentment,

gnats are sawing the air,
the sun plates your back,
salt singes your eyes
and a crab, the brush in its pincer,
scrapes the white sand of canvas,

as the sea's huge eye stuns you
with the lumbering, oblique blow
of its weary, pelagic eyelid,
its jaw ruminates
on the seagrass it munches
while the lighthouse needle signals
like a stuttering compass
north north by northwest north
and your hair roars like an oven
and a cloud passes,
till the landscape settles on
a horizon humming with balance,
and like a tired sitter
the world shifts its weight.

Remember Vincent, saint
of all sunstroke, remember
Paul, their heads
plated with fire!
The sun explodes into irises,
the shadows are crossing like crows,
they settle, clawing the hair,
yellow is screaming.

Dear Theo, I shall go mad.

Is that where it lies,
in the light of that leaf, the glint
of some gully, in a day
glinting with mica, in that rock
that shatters in slate,
in that flashing buckle of ocean?

The skull is sucked dry as a seed,
the landscape is finished.
The ants blacken it, signing.
Round the roar of an oven, the gnats
hiss their finical contradiction.
Nature is a fire,
through the door of this landscape
I have entered a furnace.

I rise, ringing with sunstroke!

The foreground lurches up drunkenly,
the cold sea is coiled in your gut,
the sky's ring dilates, dilates, and
the tongue tastes sand,
the mouth is sour with failure,
the hair on your nape,
spiders running over your wrist,
stirs like trees on the edge of that ridge,
you have eaten nothing but this landscape
all day, from daybreak to noon and past noon
the acrid greens and ochres
rust in the gut.
The stomach heaves, look away.
Your lashes settle like crows.

I have toiled all of life for this failure.
Beyond this frame, deceptive, indifferent,
nature returns to its work,
behind the square of blue you have cut from that sky,
another life, real, indifferent, resumes.
Let the hole heal itself.
The window is shut.
The eyelids cool in the shade.
Nothing will show after this, nothing
except the frame which you carry in your sealed, surrendering eyes.

II

Where did I fail? I could draw,
I was disciplined, humble, I rendered
the visible world that I saw
exactly, yet it hindered me, for
in every surface I sought
the paradoxical flash of an instant
in which every facet was caught
in a crystal of ambiguities,
I hoped that both disciplines might
by painful accretion cohere
and finally ignite,
but I lived in a different gift,
its element metaphor,
while Gregorias would draw
with the linear elation of an eel
one muscle in one thought,
my hand was crabbed by that style,
this epoch, that school
or the next, it shared
the translucent soul of the fish, while
Gregorias abandoned apprenticeship
to the errors of his own soul,
it was classic versus romantic
perhaps, it was water and fire,
and how often my hand betrayed
creeping across the white sand,
poor crab, its circuitous instinct
to fasten on what it seized,
but I was his runner, I paced him,
I admired the explosion of impulse,
I envied and understood
his mountainous derision
at this sidewise crawling, this classic
condition of servitude.
His work was grotesque, but whole,
and however bad it became

it was his, he possessed
aboriginal force and it came
as the carver comes out of the wood.
Now, every landscape we entered
was already signed with his name.

CHAPTER 14

—Anna awaking

I

When the oil green water glows but doesn't catch,
only its burnish, something wakes me early,
draws me out breezily to the pebbly shelf
of shallows where the water chuckles
and the ribbed boats sleep like children,
buoyed on their creases. I have nothing to do,
the burnished kettle is already polished,
to see my own blush burn,
and the last thing the breeze needs is my exhilaration.

I lie to my body with useless chores.
The ducks, if they ever slept, waddle knowingly.
The pleats of the shallows are neatly creased
and decorous and processional,
they arrive at our own harbour from the old hospital
across the harbour. When the first canoe,
silent, will not wave at me,
I understand, we are acknowledging
our separate silences, as the one silence,
I know that they know my peace as I know theirs.
I am amazed that the wind is tirelessly fresh.
The wind is older than the world.

It is always one thing at a time.
Now, it is always girlish.
I am happy enough to see it as a kind
of dimpled, impish smiling.
When the sleep-smelling house stirs
to that hoarse first cough, that child's first cry,
that rumbled, cavernous questioning of my mother,
I come out of the cave

like the wind emerging,
like a bride, to her first morning.

I shall make coffee.
The light, like a fiercer dawn,
will singe the downy edges of my hair,
and the heat will plate my forehead till it shines.
Its sweat will share the excitement of my cunning.
Mother, I am in love.
Harbour, I am waking.
I know the pain in your budding, nippled limes,
I know why your limbs shake, windless, pliant trees.
I shall grow grey as this light.
The first flush will pass.
But there will always be morning,
and I shall have this fever waken me,
whoever I lie to, lying close to, sleeping
like a ribbed boat in the last shallows of night.

But even if I love not him but the world,
and the wonder of the world in him, of him in the world,
and the wonder that he makes the world waken to me,
I shall never grow old in him,
I shall always be morning to him,
and I must walk and be gentle as morning.
Without knowing it, like the wind,
that cannot see her face,
the serene humility of her exultation,
that having straightened the silk sea smooth, having noticed
that the comical ducks ignore her, that
the childish pleats of the shallows are set straight,
that everyone, even the old, sleeps in innocence,
goes in nothing, naked, as I would be,
if I had her nakedness, her transparent body.
The bells garland my head. I could be happy,
just because today is Sunday. No, for more.

II

Then Sundays, smiling, carried in both hands
a towelled dish bubbling with the good life
whose fervour, steaming, beaded her clear brow,
from which damp skeins were brushed,
and ladled out her fullness to the brim.
And all those faded prints that pressed their scent
on her soft, house-warm body
glowed from her flesh with work,
her hands that held the burnish of dry hillsides
freckled with firelight,
hours that ripened till the fullest hour
could burst with peace.

"Let's go for a little walk," she said, one afternoon,
"I'm in a walking mood." Near the lagoon,
dark water's lens had made the trees one wood
arranged to frame this pair whose pace
unknowingly measured loss,
each face was set towards its character.
Where they now stood, others before had stood,
the same lens held them, the repeated wood,
then there grew on each one
the self-delighting, self-transfiguring stone
stare of the demi-god.
Stunned by their images they strolled on, content
that the black film of water kept the print
of their locked images when they passed on.

III

And which of them in time would be betrayed
was never questioned by that poetry
which breathed within the evening naturally,
but by the noble treachery of art
that looks for fear when it is least afraid,

that coldly takes the pulse-beat of the heart
in happiness; that praised its need to die
to the bright candour of the evening sky,
that preferred love to immortality;
so every step increased that subtlety
which hoped that their two bodies could be made
one body of immortal metaphor.
The hand she held already had betrayed
them by its longing for describing her.

CHAPTER 20

—Down their carved names
   the raindrop ploughs
         —HARDY

I

Smug, behind glass, we watch the passengers,
like cattle breaking, disembark.
One life, one marriage later I watched Gregorias stride
across the tarmac at Piarco, that familiar lope
that melancholy hunter's stride
seemed broken, part of the herd.
                     Something inside
me broke subtly, like a vein. I saw him grope
desperately, vaguely for his friend,
for something which a life's bewilderment could claim
as stable. I shouted, "Apilo!"
Panic and wonder struggled for the grin.

"O the years, O . . ."
                     The highway canes unrolled in
silence past the car glass, like glass
the years divided. We fished for the right level, shrill,
hysterical, until, when it subsided,
a cautionary silence glazed each word.
Was he as broken down as I had heard,
driven deep in debt,
unable to hold down a job, painting so badly
that those who swore his genius vindicated
everything once, now saw it as a promise never kept?
Viciously, near tears, I wished him dead.

I wished him a spiteful martyrdom, in revenge
for their contempt, their tiring laughter.
After I told him, he laughed and said, "I tried it once.

"One morning I lay helplessly in bed,
everything drained, gone. The children crying.
I couldn't take any more. I had dreamed of dying.
I sent for Peggy, you remember her?
She's in the States now. Anyhow,
I sent her to the bathroom for a blade . . .
When she had brought it, I asked her to go.
I lay there with the razor blade in my hand . . .
I tried to cut my wrist . . . I don't know why
I stopped. I wanted very, very much to die . . .
Only some nights before, I had had a dream . . .
I dreamt . . ."
                    And what use what he dreamt?
"We lived in a society which denied itself heroes"
(Naipaul), poor scarred carapace
shining from those abrasions it has weathered,
wearing his own humility like a climate,
a man exhausted, racked by his own strength,
Gregorias, I saw, had entered life.

They shine, they shine,
such men. After the vision
of their own self-exhaustion bores them,
till, slowly unsurprised at their own greatness,
needing neither martyrdom nor magnificence,
"I see, I see," is what Gregorias cried,
living within that moment where he died.

Re-reading Pasternak's *Safe Conduct*
as always again when life
startles under the lamplight,
I saw him brutally as Mayakovsky,
nostalgia, contempt raged for his death,
and the old choir of frogs,
those spinsterish, crackling cicadas.
Yet, even in such books
the element has burnt out,
honour and revelation are

a votive flame, and what's left
is too much like a wreath,
a smoky, abrupt recollection.
I write of a man whom life,
not death or memory, grants fame,
in my own pantheon, so, while
this fiery particle
thrives fiercely in another,
even if fuelled by liquor
to venerate the good,
honour the humbly great,
to render in "an irresponsible citizen"
the simple flame.

Too late, too late.

II

The rain falls like knives
on the kitchen floor.
The sky's heavy drawer
was pulled out too suddenly.
The raw season is on us.

For days it has huddled on the kitchen sill,
tense, a smoke-and-orange kitten
flexing its haunches,
coiling its yellow scream,
and now, it springs.
Nimble fingers of lightning
have picked the watershed,
the wires fling their beads.
Tears, like slow crystal beetles, crawl the pane.

On such days, when the postman's bicycle
whirrs drily like the locust
that brings rain, I dread my premonitions.

A grey spot, a waterdrop
blisters my hand.
A sodden letter thunders in my hand.
The insect gnaws steadily at its leaf,
an eaten letter crumbles in my hand,
as he once held my drawing to his face,
as though dusk were myopic, not his gaze.

"Harry has killed himself. He was found dead
in a house in the country. He was dead for two days."

III

The fishermen, like thieves, shake out their silver,
the lithe knives wriggle on the drying sand.
They go about their work,
their chronicler has gone about his work.

At Garand, at Piaille, at L'Anse la Verdure,
the sky is grey as pewter, without meaning.
It thunders and the kitten scuttles back
into the kitchen bin
of coal, its tines sheathing, unsheathing,
its yellow eyes the colour of fool's gold.

He had left this note.
No meaning, and no meaning.

All day, on the tin roofs
the rain berates the poverty of life,
all day the sunset bleeds like a cut wrist.

IV

Well, there you have your seasons, prodigy!
For instance, the autumnal fall of bodies,

deaths, like a comic, brutal repetition,
and in the Book of Hours, that seemed so far,
the light and amber of another life,
there is a Reaper busy about his wheat,
one who stalks nearer, and will not look up
from the scythe's swish in the orange evening grass,
and the fly at the font of your ear
sings, Hurry, hurry!
Never to set eyes on this page,
ah, Harry, never to read our names,
like a stone blurred with tears I could not read
among the pilgrims, and the mooning child
staring from the window of the high studio.

Brown, balding, with a lacertilian
jut to his underlip,
with spectacles thick as a glass paperweight
and squat, blunt fingers,
waspish, austere, swift with asperities,
with a dimpled pot for a belly from the red clay of Piaille.
Eyes like the glint of sea-smoothed bottle glass,
his knee-high khaki stockings,
brown shoes lacquered even in desolation.

People entered his understanding
like a wayside country church,
they had built him themselves.
It was they who had smoothed the wall
of his clay-coloured forehead,
who made of his rotundity an earthy
useful object
holding the clear water of their simple troubles,
he who returned their tribal names
to the adze, mattock, midden, and cooking pot.

A tang of white rum on the tongue of the mandolin,
a young bay, parting its mouth,
a heron silently named or a night-moth,

or the names of villages plaited into one map,
in the evocation of scrubbed back-yard smoke,
and he is a man no more
but the fervour and intelligence
of a whole country.

Leonce, Placide, Alcindor,
Dominic, from whose plane vowels were shorn
odorous as forest,
ask the charcoal-burner to look up
with his singed eyes,
ask the lip-cracked fisherman three miles at sea
with nothing between him and Dahomey's coast
to dip rainwater over his parched boards
for Monsieur Simmons, *pour* Msieu Harry Simmons,
let the husker on his pyramid of coconuts
rest on his tree.

Blow out the eyes in the unfinished portraits.

And the old woman who danced
with a spine like the "glory cedar,"
so lissome that her veins bulged evenly
upon the tightened drumskin of the earth,
her feet nimbler than the drummer's fingers,
let her sit in her corner and become evening
for a man the colour of her earth,
for a cracked claypot full of idle brushes,
and the tubes curl and harden,
except the red,
except the virulent red!

His island forest open and enclose him
like a rare butterfly between its leaves.

CHAPTER 22

I

Miasma, acedia, the enervations of damp,
as the teeth of the mould gnaw, greening the carious stump
of the beaten, corrugated silver of the marsh light,
where the red heron hides, without a secret,
as the cordage of mangrove tightens
bland water to bland sky
heavy and sodden as canvas,
where the pirogue foundered with its caved-in stomach
(a hulk, trying hard to look like
a paleolithic, half-gnawed memory of pre-history)
as the too green acid grasses set the salt teeth on edge,
acids and russets and water-coloured water,
let the historian go mad there
from thirst. Slowly the water rat takes up its reed pen
and scribbles. Leisurely, the egret
on the mud tablet stamps its hieroglyph.

The explorer stumbles out of the bush crying out for myth.
The tired slave vomits his past.
The Mediterranean accountant, with the nose of the water rat,
ideograph of the egret's foot,
calculates his tables,
his eyes reddening like evening in the glare of the brass lamp;
the Chinese grocer's smile is leaden with boredom:
so many lbs. of cod,
                so many bales of biscuits,
on spiked shop paper,
the mummified odour of onions,
spikenard, and old Pharaohs peeling like onionskin
to the archaeologist's finger—all that
is the Muse of history. Potsherds,
and the crusted amphora of cutthroats.

Like old leather,
tannic, stinking, peeling in a self-contemptuous
curl away from itself,
the yellowing poems, the spiked brown paper,
the myth of the golden Carib,
like a worn-out film,
the lyrical arrow in the writhing Arawak maiden
broken under the leaf-light.
                              The astigmatic geologist
stoops, with the crouch of the heron,
deciphering—not a sign.
All of the epics are blown away with the leaves,
blown with the careful calculations on brown paper;
these were the only epics: the leaves.

No horsemen here, no cuirasses
crashing, no fork-bearded Castilians,
only the narrow, silvery creeks of sadness
like the snail's trail,
only the historian deciphering, in invisible ink,
its patient slime,
no cataracts abounding down gorges
like bolts of lace,
while the lizards are taking a million years to change,
and the lopped head of the coconut rolls to gasp on the sand,
its mouth open at the very moment
of forgetting its name.

That child who sets his half-shell afloat
in the brown creek that is Rampanalgas River—
my son first, then two daughters—
towards the roar of waters,
towards the Atlantic with a dead almond leaf for a sail,
with a twig for a mast,
was, like his father, this child,
a child without history, without knowledge of its pre-world,
only the knowledge of water runnelling rocks,
and the desperate whelk that grips the rock's outcrop

like a man whom the waves can never wash overboard;
that child who puts the shell's howl to his ear,
hears nothing, hears everything
that the historian cannot hear, the howls
of all the races that crossed the water,
the howls of grandfathers drowned
in that intricately swivelled Babel,
hears the fellaheen, the Madrasi, the Mandingo, the Ashanti,
yes, and hears also the echoing green fissures of Canton,
and thousands without longing for this other shore
by the mud tablets of the Indian provinces,
robed ghostly white and brown, the twigs of uplifted hands,
of manacles, mantras, of a thousand kaddishes,
whorled, drilling into the shell,
see, in the evening light by the saffron, sacred Benares,
how they are lifting like herons,
robed ghostly white and brown,
and the crossing of water has erased their memories.
And the sea, which is always the same,
accepts them.

And the shore, which is always the same,
accepts them.

In the shallop of the shell,
in the round prayer,
in the palate of the conch,
in the dead sail of the almond leaf
are all of the voyages.

II

And those who gild cruelty,
who read from the entrails of disembowelled Aztecs
the colours of Hispanic glory
greater than Greece,
greater than Rome,

than the purple of Christ's blood,
the golden excrement on barbarous altars
of their beaked and feathered king,
and the feasts of human flesh,
those who remain fascinated,
in attitudes of prayer,
by the festering roses made from their fathers' manacles,
or upraise their silver chalices flecked with vomit,
who see a golden, cruel, hawk-bright glory
in the conquistador's malarial eye,
crying, at least here
something happened—
they will absolve us, perhaps, if we begin again,
from what we have always known, nothing,
from that carnal slime of the garden,
from the incarnate subtlety of the snake,
from the Egyptian moment of the heron's foot
on the mud's entablature,
by this augury of ibises
flying at evening from the melting trees,
while the silver-hammered charger of the marsh light
brings towards us, again and again, in beaten scrolls,
nothing, then nothing,
and then nothing.

III

Here, rest. Rest, heaven. Rest, hell.
Patchwork, sun floor, sea floor of pebbles at Resthaven, Rampanalgas
Sick of black angst.
Too many penitential histories passing
for poems. Avoid:
                1857 Lucknow and Cawnpore.
The process of history machined through fact,
for the poet's cheap alcohol,
lines like the sugar-cane factory's mechanization of myth
ground into rubbish.

1834 slavery abolished.
A century later slavishly revived
for the nose of the water rat, for the literature of the factory,
in the masochistic veneration of
chains, and the broken rum jugs of cutthroats.
Exegesis, exegesis, writers
giving their own sons homework.

Ratoon, ratoon,
immigrant hordes downed soughing,
sickled by fever, *mal d'estomac,*
earth-eating slaves fitted with masks against despair,
not mental despondence but helminthiasis.

Pour la dernière fois, nommez! Nommez!

Abouberika Torre commonly called Joseph Samson.
Hammadi Torrouke commonly called Louis Modeste.
Mandingo sergeants offered Africa back,
the boring process of repatriation,
while to the indentured Indians
the plains of Caroni seemed like the Gangetic plain,
our fathers' bones. Which father?

Burned in the pyre of the sun.
On the ashpit of the sand.
Also you, Grandfather. Rest, heaven, rest, hell.
I sit in the roar of that sun
like a lotus yogi folded on his bed of coals,
my head is circled with a ring of fire.

IV

O sun, on that morning,
did I not mutter towards your
holy, repetitive resurrection, "Hare,
hare Krishna," and then, politely,

"Thank you, life"? Not
to enter the knowledge of God
but to know that His name
had lain too familiar on my tongue,
as this one would say "bread,"
or "sun," or "wine," I staggered,
shaken at my remorse, as one
would say "bride," or "bread,"
or "sun," or "wine," to believe—
and that you would rise again,
when I am not here, to catch
the air afire, that you need not
look for me, or need this prayer.

     v

So, I shall repeat myself,
prayer, same prayer, towards fire, same fire,
as the sun repeats itself and the thundering waters

for what else is there
but books, books and the sea,
verandahs and the pages of the sea,
to write of the wind and the memory of wind-whipped hair
in the sun, the colour of fire?

I was eighteen then, now I am forty-one,
I have had a serpent for companion,
I was a heart full of knives,
but, my son, my sun,

holy is Rampanalgas and its high-circling hawks,
holy are the rusted, tortured, rust-caked, blind almond trees,
your great-grandfather's, and your father's torturing limbs,
holy the small, almond-leaf-shadowed bridge
by the small red shop, where everything smells of salt,
and holiest the break of the blue sea below the trees,

and the rock that takes blows on its back
and is more rock,
and the tireless hoarse anger of the waters
by which I can walk calm, a renewed, exhausted man,
balanced at its edge by the weight of two dear daughters.

VI

Holy were you, Margaret,
and holy our calm.
What can I do now

but sit in the sun to burn
with an ageing mirror that blinds,
combing, uncombing my hair—

escape? No, I am inured
only to the real, which
burns. Like the flesh

of my children afire.
Inured. Inward. As rock,
I wish, as the real

rock I make real,
to have burnt out desire,
lust, except for the sun

with her corona of fire.
Anna, I wanted to grow white-haired
as the wave, with a wrinkled

brown rock's face, salted,
seamed, an old poet,
facing the wind

and nothing, which is,
the loud world in his mind.

From

SEA GRAPES

(1 9 7 6)

SEA GRAPES

That sail which leans on light,
tired of islands,
a schooner beating up the Caribbean

for home, could be Odysseus,
home-bound on the Aegean;
that father and husband's

longing, under gnarled sour grapes, is
like the adulterer hearing Nausicaa's name
in every gull's outcry.

This brings nobody peace. The ancient war
between obsession and responsibility
will never finish and has been the same

for the sea-wanderer or the one on shore
now wriggling on his sandals to walk home,
since Troy sighed its last flame,

and the blind giant's boulder heaved the trough
from whose groundswell the great hexameters come
to the conclusions of exhausted surf.

The classics can console. But not enough.

ADAM'S SONG

The adulteress stoned to death
is killed in our own time
by whispers, by the breath
that films her flesh with slime.

The first was Eve,
who horned God for the serpent,
for Adam's sake—which makes
everyone guilty or Eve innocent.

Nothing has changed,
for men still sing the song that Adam sang
against the world he lost to vipers,

the song to Eve
against his own damnation;
he sang it in the evening of the world

with the lights coming on in the eyes
of panthers in the peaceable kingdom
and his death coming out of the trees,

he sings it, frightened
of the jealousy of God and at the price
of his own death.

The song ascends to God, who wipes His eyes:

"Heart, you are in my heart as the bird rises,
heart, you are in my heart while the sun sleeps,
heart, you lie still in me as the dew is,
you weep within me, as the rain weeps."

THE CLOUD

And, laterally,
to Adam's pulsing eye,
the erect ridges would throb and recede,

a sigh under the fig tree and a sky
deflating to the serpent's punctured hiss,
repeating you will die.

The woman lay still as the settling mountains.
There was another silence,
all was thick with it;

the clouds given a mortal destination,
the silent shudder from the broken branch
where the sap dripped

from the torn tree.
When she, his death,
turned on her side and slept,
the breath he drew was his first real breath.

What left the leaves,
the phosphorescent air,
was both God and the serpent leaving him.
Neither could curse or bless.

Pollen was drifting to the woman's hair,
his eye felt brighter,
a cloud's slow shadow slowly covered them,

and, as it moved, he named it Tenderness.

There's the wide desert, but no one marches
except in the pads of old caravans,
there is the ocean, but the keels incise
the precise, old parallels,
there's the blue sea above the mountains
but they scratch the same lines
in the jet trails—
so the politicians plod
without imagination, circling
the same sombre garden
with its fountain dry in the forecourt,
the grigri palms desiccating
dung pods like goats,
the same lines rule the White Papers,
the same steps ascend Whitehall,
and only the name of the fool changes
under the plumed white cork-hat
for the Independence parades,
revolving around, in calypso,
to the brazen joy of the tubas.

Why are the eyes of the beautiful
and unmarked children
in the uniforms of the country
bewildered and shy,
why do they widen in terror
of the pride drummed into their minds?
Were they truer, the old songs,
when the law lived far away,
when the veiled queen, her girth
as comfortable as cushions,
upheld the orb with its stern admonitions?
We wait for the changing of statues,
for the change of parades.

Here he comes now, here he comes!
Papa! Papa! With his crowd,
the sleek, waddling seals of his Cabinet,
trundling up to the dais,
as the wind puts its tail between
the cleft of the mountain, and a wave
coughs once, abruptly.
Who will name this silence
respect? Those forced, hoarse hosannas
awe? That tin-ringing tune
from the pumping, circling horns
the New World? Find a name
for that look on the faces
of the electorate. Tell me
how it all happened, and why
I said nothing.

THE BRIGHT FIELD

My nerves steeled against the power of London,
I hurried home that evening, with the sense
we all have, of the crowd's hypocrisy,
to feel my rage, turned on in self-defence,
bear mercy for the anonymity
of every self humbled by massive places,
and I, who moved against a bitter sea,
was moved by the light on Underground-bound faces.

Their sun that would not set was going down
on their flushed faces, brickwork like a kiln,
on pillar-box-bright buses between trees,
with the compassion of calendar art—
like walking sheaves of harvest, the quick crowd
thickened in separate blades of cane or wheat
from factories and office doors conveyed
to one end by the loud belt of the street.
And that end brings its sadness, going in
by Underground, by cab, by bullock-cart,
and lances us with punctual, maudlin
pity down lanes or cane-fields, till the heart,
seeing, like dark canes, the river-spires sharpen,
feels an involuntary bell begin
to toll for everything, even in London,
heart of our history, original sin.

The vision that brought Samuel Palmer peace,
that stoked Blake's fury at her furnaces,
flashes from doormen's buttons and the rocks
around Balandra. These slow belfry-strokes—
cast in the pool of London, from which swallows
rise in wide rings, and from their bright field, rooks—
mark the same beat by which a pelican goes
across Salybia as the tide lowers.

SAINTE LUCIE

I
The Villages

Laborie, Choiseul, Vieux Fort, Dennery,
from these sun-bleached villages
where the church bell caves in the sides
of one grey-scurfed shack that is shuttered
with warped boards, with rust,
with crabs crawling under the house-shadow
where the children played house;
a net rotting among cans, the sea-net
of sunlight trolling the shallows
catching nothing all afternoon,
from these I am growing no nearer
to what secret eluded the children
under the house-shade, in the far bell, the noon's
stunned amethystine sea,
something always being missed
between the floating shadow and the pelican
in the smoke from over the next bay
in that shack on the lip of the sandspit
whatever the seagulls cried out for
through the grey drifting ladders of rain
and the great grey tree of the waterspout,
for which the dolphins kept diving, that
should have rounded the day.

II

Pomme-arac,
otaheite apple,
pomme cythère,
pomme granate,
moubain,

z'anananas
the pineapple's
Aztec helmet,
pomme,
I have forgotten
what pomme for
the Irish potato,
cerise,
the cherry,
z'aman
sea-almonds
by the crisp
sea-bursts,
au bord de la 'ouvière.
Come back to me,
my language.
Come back,
cacao,
grigri,
solitaire,
ciseau
the scissor-bird
no nightingales
except, once,
in the indigo mountains
of Jamaica, blue depth,
deep as coffee,
flicker of pimento,
the shaft light
on a yellow ackee
the bark alone bare
jardins
en montagnes
en haut betassion
the wet leather reek
of the hill donkey.

Evening opens at
a text of fireflies,
in the mountain huts
ti cailles betassion
candles,
candleflies
the black night bending
cups in its hard palms
cool thin water
this is important water,
important?
imported?
water is important
also very important
the red rust drum
the evening deep
as coffee
the morning powerful
important coffee
the villages shut
all day in the sun.

In the empty schoolyard
teacher dead today
the fruit rotting
yellow on the ground,
dyes from Gauguin
the pomme-arac dyes
the earth purple,
the ochre roads
still waiting in the sun
for my shadow,
Oh, so you is Walcott?
you is Roddy brother?
Teacher Alix son?
and the small rivers
with important names.

And the important corporal
in the country station
en betassion
looking towards the thick
green slopes of cocoa
the sun that melts
the asphalt at noon,
and the woman in the shade
of the breadfruit bent over
the lip of the valley,
below her, blue-green
the lost, lost valleys
of sugar, the bus rides,
the fields of bananas
the tanker still rusts
in the lagoon at Roseau,
and around what corner
was uttered a single
yellow leaf,
from the frangipani
a tough bark, reticent,
but when it flowers
delivers hard lilies,
pungent, recalling

Martina, or Eunice
or Lucilla,
who comes down the steps
with the cool, side flow
as spring water eases
over shelves of rock
in some green ferny hole
by the road in the mountains,
her smile like the whole country,
her smell, earth,
red-brown earth, her armpits
a reaping, her arms
saplings, an old woman

that she is now,
with other generations
of daughters flowing
down the steps,
gens betassion,
belle ti fille betassion,
until their teeth go,
and all the rest.

O Martinas, Lucillas,
I'm a wild golden apple
that will burst with love
of you and your men,
those I never told enough
with my young poet's eyes
crazy with the country,
generations going,
generations gone,
moi c'est gens Ste. Lucie.
C'est la moi sorti;
is there that I born.

III
Iona: Mabouya Valley

*St. Lucian conte, or narrative Creole song, heard on the back
of an open truck travelling to Vieux Fort, some years ago*

Ma Kilman, Bon Dieu kai punir 'ous,
Pour qui raison parcequ' ous entrer trop religion.
Oui, l'autre coté, Bon Dieu kai benir 'ous,
Bon Dieu kai benir 'ous parcequi 'ous faire charité l'argent.

Corbeau aille Curaçao,
i' voyait l'argent ba 'ous,
ous prend l'argent cela,

ous mettait lui en cabaret.
Ous pas ka lire, ecrire, 'ous pas ka parler Anglais,
ous tait supposer ca; cabaret pas ni benefice.
L'heure Corbeau devirait,
l'tait ni, l' tait ni l'argent,
L'heure i' rivait ici.
Oui, maman! Corbeau kai fou!

Iona dit Corbeau, pendant 'ous tait Curaçao,
Moi fait deux 'tits mamaille, venir garder si c'est ca 'ous.
Corbeau criait: "Mama! Bonsoir, messieurs, mesdames,
lumer lampe-la ba moi,
pour moi garder ces mamailles-la!"
Corbeau virait dire: "Moi save toutes negres ka semble.
i peut si pas ca moin,
moi kai soigner ces mamailles-la!"

Oui, Corbeau partit, Corbeau descend Roseau,
allait chercher travail, pourqui 'peut soigner ces mamailles-la.
Iona dit Corbeau, pas tait descendre Roseau.

Mais i' descend Roseau, jamettes Roseau tomber derriere-i'.
Philippe Mago achetait un sax bai Corbeau,
i' pas ni temps jouer sax-la,
saxman comme lui prendre la vie-lui.

Samedi bon matin, Corbeau partit descendre en ville.
Samedi apres-midi, nous 'tendre la mort Corbeau.
Ca fait moi la peine, oui, ca brulait coeur-moin;
ca penetrait moin, l'heure moin 'tendre la mort Corbeau.

Iona dit comme-ca: ca qui fait lui la peine,
ca qui brulait coeur-lui, saxophone Corbeau pas jouer.
Moin 'tendre un corne cornait
a sur bord roseaux-a.
Moi dit: "Doux-doux, moin kai chercher
volants ba 'ous."
L'heure moin 'rivait la, moin fait raconte epi Corbeau.

I' dit: "Corne-la qui cornait-a,
c'est Iona ka cornait moin."

Guitar man la ka dire:
"Nous tous les deux c'est guitar man,
pas prendre ca pour un rien,
c'est meme beat-la nous ka chember."

Iona mariée, Dimanche a quatre heures.
Mardi, a huit heures, i' aille l'hopital.
I'fait un bombe, mari-lui cassait bras-lui.
L'heure moi joindre maman-ous,
Moin kai conter toute ca 'ous 'ja faire moin.
Iona!
(N'ai dire maman-ous!)
Iona!
(Ous pas ka 'couter moin!)

Trois jours, trois nuits
Iona bouillit, Iona pas chuitte.
(N'ai dit maman-i' ca.)
Toute moune ka dit Iona tourner,
C'est pas tourner Iona tourner,
mauvais i' mauvais,
Iona!

IV
Iona: Mabouya Valley

[*for Eric Branford*]

Ma Kilman, God will punish you,
for the reason that you've got too much religion.
On the other hand, God will bless you,
God will bless you because of your charity.

Corbeau went to Curaçao,
he sent you money back,
you took the same money
and put it in a rumshop.
You can't read, you can't write, you can't speak English,
you should know that rum-shops make no profit.
When Corbeau came back,
he had, yes he had money,
when he arrived back here.
Yes, Mama, Corbeau'll go crazy!

Iona told Corbeau, while you were in Curaçao,
I made two little children, come and see if they're yours.
Corbeau cried out, "Mama! Good night, ladies and gentlemen,
light the lamp there for me,
for me to look at these kids!"
Corbeau came back and said, "I know niggers resemble,
they may or may not be mine,
I'll mind them all the same!"

Ah yes, Corbeau then left, he went down to Roseau,
he went to look for work, to mind the two little ones.
Iona told Corbeau, don't go down to Roseau.

But he went to Roseau, and Roseau's whores fell on him.
Philippe Mago brought Corbeau a saxophone,
he had no time to play the sax,
a saxman just like him took away his living.

Saturday morning early, Corbeau goes into town.
Saturday afternoon we hear Corbeau is dead.
That really made me sad, that really burnt my heart;
that really went through me when I heard Corbeau was dead.

Iona said like this: it made her sorry too,
it really burnt her heart, that the saxophone will never play.

I heard a horn blowing
by the river reeds down there.
"Sweetheart," I said, "I'll go looking
for flying fish for you."
When I got there, I came across Corbeau.
He said: "That horn you heard
was Iona horning me."

The guitar man's saying:
"We both are guitar men,
don't take it for anything,
we both holding the same beat."

Iona got married, Sunday at four o'clock.
Tuesday, by eight o'clock, she's in the hospital.
She made a fare, her husband broke her arm.
When I meet your mother,
I'll tell what you did me.
Iona!
(I'll tell your mama!)
Iona!
(You don't listen to me!)

Three days and three nights
Iona boiled, she's still not cooked.
(I'll tell her mother that.)
They say Iona's changed,
it isn't changed Iona's changed,
she's wicked, wicked, that's all,
Iona!

V

For the Altarpiece of the Roseau Valley Church, St. Lucia

1

The chapel, as the pivot of this valley,
round which whatever is rooted loosely turns—
men, women, ditches, the revolving fields
of bananas, the secondary roads—
draws all to it, to the altar
and the massive altarpiece,
like a dull mirror, life
repeated there,
the common life outside
and the other life it holds;
a good man made it.

Two earth-brown labourers
dance the botay in it, the drum sounds under
the earth, the heavy foot.

                              This is a rich valley,
It is fat with things.
Its roads radiate like aisles from the altar towards
those acres of bananas, towards
leaf-crowded mountains
rain-bellied clouds
in haze, in iron heat;

                              This is a cursed valley,
ask the broken mules, the swollen children,
ask the dried women, their gap-toothed men,
ask the parish priest, who, in the altarpiece,
carries a replica of the church,
ask the two who could be Eve and Adam dancing.

2

Five centuries ago
in the time of Giotto
this altar might have had
in one corner, when God was young,
St. Omer me fecit aetat, whatever his own age now,
Gloria Dei and to God's Mother also.

It is signed with music.
It turns the whole island.
You have to imagine it empty on a Sunday afternoon
between adorations
Nobody can see it and it is there,
nobody adores the two who could be Eve and Adam dancing.

A Sunday at three o'clock
when the real Adam and Eve have coupled
and lie in rechristening sweat

his sweat on her still breasts,
her sweat on his panelled torso
that hefts bananas
that has killed snakes
that has climbed out of rivers,

now, as on the furred tops of the hills,
a breeze moving the hairs on his chest
on a Sunday at three o'clock
when the snake pours itself
into a chalice of leaves.

The sugar factory is empty.

Nobody picks bananas,
no trucks raising dust on their way to Vieux Fort,
no helicopter spraying

the mosquito's banjo, yes,
and the gnat's violin, okay,

okay, not absolute Adamic silence,
the valley of Roseau is not the Garden of Eden,
and those who inhabit it are not in heaven,

so there are little wires of music
some marron up in the hills, by Aux Lyons,
some christening.

A boy banging a tin by the river,
with the river trying to sleep.
But nothing can break that silence,

which comes from the depth of the world,
from whatever one man believes he knows of God
and the suffering of his kind,

it comes from the wall of the altarpiece
ST. OMER AD GLORIAM DEI FECIT
in whatever year of his suffering.

3

After so many bottles of white rum in a pile,
after the flight of so many little fishes
from the brush that is the finger of St. Francis,

after the deaths
of as many names as you want,
Iona, Julian, Ti-Nomme, Cacao,
like the death of the cane crop in Roseau Valley, St. Lucia.

After five thousand novenas
and the idea of the Virgin
coming and going like a little lamp,

after all that,
your faith like a canoe at evening coming in,
like a relative who is tired of America,
like a woman coming back to your house,

that sang in the ropes of your wrist
when you lifted this up;
so that, from time to time, on Sundays

between adorations, one might see,
if one were there, and not there,
looking in at the windows

the real faces of angels.

VOLCANO

Joyce was afraid of thunder,
but lions roared at his funeral
from the Zurich zoo.
Was it Zurich or Trieste?
No matter. These are legends, as much
as the death of Joyce is a legend,
or the strong rumour that Conrad
is dead, and that *Victory* is ironic.
On the edge of the night-horizon
from this beach house on the cliffs
there are now, till dawn,
two glares from the miles-out-
at-sea derricks; they are like
the glow of the cigar
and the glow of the volcano
at *Victory*'s end.
One could abandon writing
for the slow-burning signals
of the great, to be, instead,
their ideal reader, ruminative,
voracious, making the love of masterpieces
superior to attempting
to repeat or outdo them,
and be the greatest reader in the world.
At least it requires awe,
which has been lost to our time;
so many people have seen everything,
so many people can predict,
so many refuse to enter the silence
of victory, the indolence
that burns at the core,
so many are no more than
erect ash, like the cigar,
so many take thunder for granted.
How common is the lightning,

how lost the leviathans
we no longer look for!
There were giants in those days.
In those days they made good cigars.
I must read more carefully.

SEA CANES

Half my friends are dead.
I will make you new ones, said earth.
No, give me them back, as they were, instead,
with faults and all, I cried.

Tonight I can snatch their talk
from the faint surf's drone
through the canes, but I cannot walk

on the moonlit leaves of ocean
down that white road alone,
or float with the dreaming motion

of owls leaving earth's load.
O earth, the number of friends you keep
exceeds those left to be loved.

The sea canes by the cliff flash green and silver;
they were the seraph lances of my faith,
but out of what is lost grows something stronger

that has the rational radiance of stone,
enduring moonlight, further than despair,
strong as the wind, that through dividing canes

brings those we love before us, as they were,
with faults and all, not nobler, just there.

MIDSUMMER, TOBAGO

Broad sun-stoned beaches.

White heat.
A green river.

A bridge,
scorched yellow palms

from the summer-sleeping house
drowsing through August.

Days I have held,
days I have lost,

days that outgrow, like daughters,
my harbouring arms.

ODDJOB, A BULL TERRIER

You prepare for one sorrow,
but another comes.
It is not like the weather,
you cannot brace yourself,
the unreadiness is all.
Your companion, the woman,
the friend next to you,
the child at your side,
and the dog,
we tremble for them,
we look seaward and muse
it will rain.
We shall get ready for rain;
you do not connect
the sunlight altering
the darkening oleanders
in the sea-garden,
the gold going out of the palms.
You do not connect this,
the fleck of the drizzle
on your flesh,
with the dog's whimper,
the thunder doesn't frighten,
the readiness is all;
what follows at your feet
is trying to tell you
the silence is all:
it is deeper than the readiness,
it is sea-deep,
earth-deep,
love-deep.

The silence
is stronger than thunder,
we are stricken dumb and deep

as the animals who never utter love
as we do, except
it becomes unutterable
and must be said,
in a whimper,
in tears,
in the drizzle that comes to our eyes
not uttering the loved thing's name,
the silence of the dead,
the silence of the deepest buried love is
the one silence,
and whether we bear it for beast,
for child, for woman, or friend,
it is the one love, it is the same,
and it is blest
deepest by loss
it is blest, it is blest.

TO RETURN TO THE TREES

[*for John Figueroa*]

Senex, an oak.
Senex, this old sea-almond
unwincing in spray

in this geriatric grove
on the sea-road to Cumana.
To return to the trees,

to decline like this tree,
the burly oak
of Boanerges Ben Jonson!

Or am I lying
like this felled almond
when I write I look forward to age—

a gnarled poet
bearded with the whirlwind,
his metres like thunder?

It is not only the sea,
no, for on windy, green mornings
I read the changes on Morne Coco Mountain,

from flagrant sunrise
to its ashen end;
grey has grown strong to me,

it's no longer neutral,
no longer the dirty flag
of courage going under,

it is speckled with hues
like quartz, it's as
various as boredom,

grey now is a crystal
haze, a dull diamond,
stone-dusted and stoic,

grey is the heart at peace,
tougher than the warrior
as it bestrides factions,

it is the great pause
when the pillars of the temple
rest on Samson's palms

and are held, held,
that moment
when the heavy rock of the world

like a child sleeps
on the trembling shoulders of Atlas
and his own eyes close,

the toil that is balance.
Seneca, that fabled bore,
and his gnarled, laborious Latin

I can read only in fragments
of broken bark, his
heroes tempered by whirlwinds,

who see with the word
"senex," with its two eyes,
through the boles of this tree,

beyond joy,
beyond lyrical utterance,
this obdurate almond

going under the sand
with this language, slowly,
by sand grains, by centuries.

From

THE STAR-APPLE KINGDOM

(1 9 7 9)

THE SCHOONER *FLIGHT*

1 *Adios, Carenage*

In idle August, while the sea soft,
and leaves of brown islands stick to the rim
of this Caribbean, I blow out the light
by the dreamless face of Maria Concepcion
to ship as a seaman on the schooner *Flight*.
Out in the yard turning grey in the dawn,
I stood like a stone and nothing else move
but the cold sea rippling like galvanize
and the nail holes of stars in the sky roof,
till a wind start to interfere with the trees.
I pass me dry neighbour sweeping she yard
as I went downhill, and I nearly said:
"Sweep soft, you witch, 'cause she don't sleep hard,"
but the bitch look through me like I was dead.
A route taxi pull up, park-lights still on.
The driver size up my bags with a grin:
"This time, Shabine, like you really gone!"
I ain't answer the ass, I simply pile in
the back seat and watch the sky burn
above Laventille pink as the gown
in which the woman I left was sleeping,
and I look in the rearview and see a man
exactly like me, and the man was weeping
for the houses, the streets, that whole fucking island.

Christ have mercy on all sleeping things!
From that dog rotting down Wrightson Road
to when I was a dog on these streets;
if loving these islands must be my load,
out of corruption my soul takes wings,
but they had started to poison my soul
with their big house, big car, big-time bohbohl,
coolie, nigger, Syrian, and French Creole,
so I leave it for them and their carnival—

I taking a sea-bath, I gone down the road.
I know these islands from Monos to Nassau,
a rusty head sailor with sea-green eyes
that they nickname Shabine, the patois for
any red nigger, and I, Shabine, saw
when these slums of empire was paradise.
I'm just a red nigger who love the sea,
I had a sound colonial education,
I have Dutch, nigger, and English in me,
and either I'm nobody, or I'm a nation.

But Maria Concepcion was all my thought
watching the sea heaving up and down
as the port side of dories, schooners, and yachts
was painted afresh by the strokes of the sun
signing her name with every reflection;
I knew when dark-haired evening put on
her bright silk at sunset, and, folding the sea,
sidled under the sheet with her starry laugh,
that there'd be no rest, there'd be no forgetting.
Is like telling mourners round the graveside
about resurrection, they want the dead back,
so I smile to myself as the bow rope untied
and the *Flight* swing seaward: "Is no use repeating
that the sea have more fish. I ain't want her
dressed in the sexless light of a seraph,
I want those round brown eyes like a marmoset, and
till the day when I can lean back and laugh,
those claws that tickled my back on sweating
Sunday afternoons, like a crab on wet sand."
As I worked, watching the rotting waves come
past the bow that scissor the sea like silk,
I swear to you all, by my mother's milk,
by the stars that shall fly from tonight's furnace,
that I loved them, my children, my wife, my home;
I loved them as poets love the poetry
that kills them, as drowned sailors the sea.

You ever look up from some lonely beach
and see a far schooner? Well, when I write
this poem, each phrase go be soaked in salt;
I go draw and knot every line as tight
as ropes in this rigging; in simple speech
my common language go be the wind,
my pages the sails of the schooner *Flight*.
But let me tell you how this business begin.

3   *Shabine Leaves the Republic*

I had no nation now but the imagination.
After the white man, the niggers didn't want me
when the power swing to their side.
The first chain my hands and apologize, "History";
the next said I wasn't black enough for their pride.
Tell me, what power, on these unknown rocks—
a spray-plane Air Force, the Fire Brigade,
the Red Cross, the Regiment, two, three police dogs
that pass before you finish bawling "Parade!"?
I met History once, but he ain't recognize me,
a parchment Creole, with warts
like an old sea-bottle, crawling like a crab
through the holes of shadow cast by the net
of a grille balcony; cream linen, cream hat.
I confront him and shout, "Sir, is Shabine!
They say I'se your grandson. You remember Grandma,
your black cook, at all?" The bitch hawk and spat.
A spit like that worth any number of words.
But that's all them bastards have left us: words.

I no longer believed in the revolution.
I was losing faith in the love of my woman.
I had seen that moment Aleksandr Blok
crystallize in *The Twelve*. Was between
the Police Marine Branch and Hotel Venezuelana
one Sunday at noon. Young men without flags

using shirts, their chests waiting for holes.
They kept marching into the mountains, and
their noise ceased as foam sinks into sand.
They sank in the bright hills like rain, every one
with his own nimbus, leaving shirts in the street,
and the echo of power at the end of the street.
Propeller-blade fans turn over the Senate;
the judges, they say, still sweat in carmine,
on Frederick Street the idlers all marching
by standing still, the Budget turns a new leaf.
In the 12:30 movies the projectors best
not break down, or you go see revolution. Aleksandr Blok
enters and sits in the third row of pit eating choc-
olate cone, waiting for a spaghetti West-
ern with Clint Eastwood and featuring Lee Van Cleef.

4   The Flight, *Passing Blanchisseuse*

Dusk. The *Flight* passing Blanchisseuse.
Gulls wheel like from a gun again,
and foam gone amber that was white,
lighthouse and star start making friends,
down every beach the long day ends,
and there, on that last stretch of sand,
on a beach bare of all but light,
dark hands start pulling in the seine
of the dark sea, deep, deep inland.

5   Shabine Encounters the Middle Passage

Man, I brisk in the galley first thing next dawn,
brewing li'l coffee; fog coil from the sea
like the kettle steaming when I put it down
slow, slow, 'cause I couldn't believe what I see:
where the horizon was one silver haze,
the fog swirl and swell into sails, so close

that I saw it was sails, my hair grip my skull,
it was horrors, but it was beautiful.
We float through a rustling forest of ships
with sails dry like paper, behind the glass
I saw men with rusty eyeholes like cannons,
and whenever their half-naked crews cross the sun,
right through their tissue, you traced their bones
like leaves against the sunlight; frigates, barquentines,
the backward-moving current swept them on,
and high on their decks I saw great admirals,
Rodney, Nelson, de Grasse, I heard the hoarse orders
they gave those Shabines, and the forest
of masts sail right through the *Flight*,
and all you could hear was the ghostly sound
of waves rustling like grass in a low wind
and the hissing weeds they trailed from the stern;
slowly they heaved past from east to west
like this round world was some cranked water wheel,
every ship pouring like a wooden bucket
dredged from the deep; my memory revolve
on all sailors before me, then the sun
heat the horizon's ring and they was mist.

Next we pass slave ships. Flags of all nations,
our fathers below deck too deep, I suppose,
to hear us shouting. So we stop shouting. Who knows
who his grandfather is, much less his name?
Tomorrow our landfall will be the Barbados.

6   *The Sailor Sings Back to the Casuarinas*

You see them on the low hills of Barbados
bracing like windbreaks, needles for hurricanes,
trailing, like masts, the cirrus of torn sails;
when I was green like them, I used to think
those cypresses, leaning against the sea,
that take the sea-noise up into their branches,

are not real cypresses but casuarinas.
Now captain just call them Canadian cedars.
But cedars, cypresses, or casuarinas,
whoever called them so had a good cause,
watching their bending bodies wail like women
after a storm, when some schooner came home
with news of one more sailor drowned again.
Once the sound "cypress" used to make more sense
than the green "casuarinas," though, to the wind
whatever grief bent them was all the same,
since they were trees with nothing else in mind
but heavenly leaping or to guard a grave;
but we live like our names and you would have
to be colonial to know the difference,
to know the pain of history words contain,
to love those trees with an inferior love,
and to believe: "Those casuarinas bend
like cypresses, their hair hangs down in rain
like sailors' wives. They're classic trees, and we,
if we live like the names our masters please,
by careful mimicry might become men."

7   *The* Flight *Anchors in Castries Harbour*

When the stars self were young over Castries,
I loved you alone and I loved the whole world.
What does it matter that our lives are different?
Burdened with the loves of our different children?
When I think of your young face washed by the wind
and your voice that chuckles in the slap of the sea?
The lights are out on La Toc promontory,
except for the hospital. Across at Vigie
the marina arcs keep vigil. I have kept my own
promise, to leave you the one thing I own,
you whom I loved first: my poetry.
We here for one night. Tomorrow, the *Flight* will be gone.

8   Fight with the Crew

It had one bitch on board, like he had me mark—
that was the cook, some Vincentian arse
with a skin like a gommier tree, red peeling bark,
and wash-out blue eyes; he wouldn't give me a ease,
like he feel he was white. Had an exercise book,
this same one here, that I was using to write
my poetry, so one day this man snatch it
from my hand, and start throwing it left and right
to the rest of the crew, bawling out, "Catch it,"
and start mincing me like I was some hen
because of the poems. Some case is for fist,
some case is for tholing pin, some is for knife—
this one was for knife. Well, I beg him first,
but he keep reading, "O my children, my wife,"
and playing he crying, to make the crew laugh;
it move like a flying fish, the silver knife
that catch him right in the plump of his calf,
and he faint so slowly, and he turn more white
than he thought he was. I suppose among men
you need that sort of thing. It ain't right
but that's how it is. There wasn't much pain,
just plenty blood, and Vincie and me best friend,
but none of them go fuck with my poetry again.

10   Out of the Depths

Next day, dark sea. A arse-aching dawn.
"Damn wind shift sudden as a woman mind."
The slow swell start cresting like some mountain range
with snow on the top.
        "Ay, Skipper, sky dark!"
"This ain't right for August."
        "This light damn strange,
this season, sky should be clear as a field."

A stingray steeplechase across the sea,
tail whipping water, the high man-o'-wars
start reeling inland, quick, quick an archery
of flying fish miss us! Vince say: "You notice?"
and a black-mane squall pounce on the sail
like a dog on a pigeon, and it snap the neck
of the *Flight* and shake it from head to tail.
"Be Jesus, I never see sea get so rough
so fast! That wind come from God back pocket!"
"Where Cap'n headin? Like the man gone blind!"
"If we's to drong, we go drong, Vince, fock-it!"
"Shabine, say your prayers, if life leave you any!"

I have not loved those that I loved enough.
Worse than the mule kick of Kick-'Em-Jenny
Channel, rain start to pelt the *Flight* between
mountains of water. If I was frighten?
The tent poles of waterspouts bracing the sky
start wobbling, clouds unstitch at the seams
and sky water drench us, and I hear myself cry,
"I'm the drowned sailor in her *Book of Dreams*."
I remembered them ghost ships, I saw me corkscrewing
to the sea-bed of sea-worms, fathom pass fathom,
my jaw clench like a fist, and only one thing
hold me, trembling, how my family safe home.
Then a strength like it seize me and the strength said:
"I from backward people who still fear God."
Let Him, in His might, heave Leviathan upward
by the winch of His will, the beast pouring lace
from his sea-bottom bed; and that was the faith
that had fade from a child in the Methodist chapel
in Chisel Street, Castries, when the whale-bell
sang service and, in hard pews ribbed like the whale,
proud with despair, we sang how our race
survive the sea's maw, our history, our peril,
and now I was ready for whatever death will.
But if that storm had strength, was in Cap'n face,
beard beading with spray, tears salting the eyes,

crucify to his post, that nigger hold fast
to that wheel, man, like the cross held Jesus,
and the wounds of his eyes like they crying for us,
and I feeding him white rum, while every crest
with Leviathan-lash make the *Flight* quail
like two criminal. Whole night, with no rest,
till red-eyed like dawn, we watch our travail
subsiding, subside, and there was no more storm.
And the noon sea get calm as Thy Kingdom Come.

11   *After the Storm*

There's a fresh light that follows a storm
while the whole sea still havoc; in its bright wake
I saw the veiled face of Maria Concepcion
marrying the ocean, then drifting away
in the widening lace of her bridal train
with white gulls her bridesmaids, till she was gone.
I wanted nothing after that day.
Across my own face, like the face of the sun,
a light rain was falling, with the sea calm.

Fall gently, rain, on the sea's upturned face
like a girl showering; make these islands fresh
as Shabine once knew them! Let every trace,
every hot road, smell like clothes she just press
and sprinkle with drizzle. I finish dream;
whatever the rain wash and the sun iron:
the white clouds, the sea and sky with one seam,
is clothes enough for my nakedness.
Though my *Flight* never pass the incoming tide
of this inland sea beyond the loud reefs
of the final Bahamas, I am satisfied
if my hand gave voice to one people's grief.
Open the map. More islands there, man,
than peas on a tin plate, all different size,
one thousand in the Bahamas alone,

from mountains to low scrub with coral keys,
and from this bowsprit, I bless every town,
the blue smell of smoke in hills behind them,
and the one small road winding down them like twine
to the roofs below; I have only one theme:

The bowsprit, the arrow, the longing, the lunging heart—
the flight to a target whose aim we'll never know,
vain search for one island that heals with its harbour
and a guiltless horizon, where the almond's shadow
doesn't injure the sand. There are so many islands!
As many islands as the stars at night
on that branched tree from which meteors are shaken
like falling fruit around the schooner *Flight*.
But things must fall, and so it always was,
on one hand Venus, on the other Mars;
fall, and are one, just as this earth is one
island in archipelagoes of stars.
My first friend was the sea. Now, is my last.
I stop talking now. I work, then I read,
cotching under a lantern hooked to the mast.
I try to forget what happiness was,
and when that don't work, I study the stars.
Sometimes is just me, and the soft-scissored foam
as the deck turn white and the moon open
a cloud like a door, and the light over me
is a road in white moonlight taking me home.
Shabine sang to you from the depths of the sea.

THE SEA IS HISTORY

Where are your monuments, your battles, martyrs?
Where is your tribal memory? Sirs,
in that grey vault. The sea. The sea
has locked them up. The sea is History.

First, there was the heaving oil,
heavy as chaos;
then, like a light at the end of a tunnel,

the lantern of a caravel,
and that was Genesis.
Then there were the packed cries,
the shit, the moaning:

Exodus.
Bone soldered by coral to bone,
mosaics
mantled by the benediction of the shark's shadow,

that was the Ark of the Covenant.
Then came from the plucked wires
of sunlight on the sea floor

the plangent harps of the Babylonian bondage,
as the white cowries clustered like manacles
on the drowned women,

and those were the ivory bracelets
of the Song of Solomon,
but the ocean kept turning blank pages

looking for History.
Then came the men with eyes heavy as anchors
who sank without tombs,

brigands who barbecued cattle,
leaving their charred ribs like palm leaves on the shore,
then the foaming, rabid maw

of the tidal wave swallowing Port Royal,
and that was Jonah,
but where is your Renaissance?

Sir, it is locked in them sea-sands
out there past the reef's moiling shelf,
where the men-o'-war floated down;

strop on these goggles, I'll guide you there myself.
It's all subtle and submarine,
through colonnades of coral,

past the gothic windows of sea-fans
to where the crusty grouper, onyx-eyed,
blinks, weighted by its jewels, like a bald queen;

and these groined caves with barnacles
pitted like stone
are our cathedrals,

and the furnace before the hurricanes:
Gomorrah. Bones ground by windmills
into marl and cornmeal,

and that was Lamentations—
that was just Lamentations,
it was not History;

then came, like scum on the river's drying lip,
the brown reeds of villages
mantling and congealing into towns,

and at evening, the midges' choirs,
and above them, the spires
lancing the side of God

as His son set, and that was the New Testament.

Then came the white sisters clapping
to the waves' progress,
and that was Emancipation—

jubilation, O jubilation—
vanishing swiftly
as the sea's lace dries in the sun,

but that was not History,
that was only faith,
and then each rock broke into its own nation;

then came the synod of flies,
then came the secretarial heron,
then came the bullfrog bellowing for a vote,

fireflies with bright ideas
and bats like jetting ambassadors
and the mantis, like khaki police,

and the furred caterpillars of judges
examining each case closely,
and then in the dark ears of ferns

and in the salt chuckle of rocks
with their sea pools, there was the sound
like a rumour without any echo

of History, really beginning.

THE SADDHU OF COUVA

[*for Kenneth Ramchand*]

When sunset, a brass gong,
vibrate through Couva,
is then I see my soul, swiftly unsheathed,
like a white cattle bird growing more small
over the ocean of the evening canes,
and I sit quiet, waiting for it to return
like a hog-cattle blistered with mud,
because, for my spirit, India is too far.
And to that gong
sometimes bald clouds in saffron robes assemble
sacred to the evening,
sacred even to Ramlochan,
singing Indian hits from his jute hammock
while evening strokes the flanks
and silver horns of his maroon taxi,
as the mosquitoes whine their evening mantras,
my friend Anopheles, on the sitar,
and the fireflies making every dusk Divali.

I knot my head with a cloud,
my white moustache bristle like horns,
my hands are brittle as the pages of Ramayana.
Once the sacred monkeys multiplied like branches
in the ancient temples; I did not miss them,
because these fields sang of Bengal,
behind Ramlochan Repairs there was Uttar Pradesh;
but time roars in my ears like a river,
old age is a conflagration
as fierce as the cane fires of crop time.
I will pass through these people like a cloud,
they will see a white bird beating the evening sea
of the canes behind Couva,
and who will point it as my soul unsheathed?

Neither the bridegroom in beads,
nor the bride in her veils,
their sacred language on the cinema hoardings.

I talked too damn much on the Couva Village Council.
I talked too softly, I was always drowned
by the loudspeakers in front of the stores
or the loudspeakers with the greatest pictures.
I am best suited to stalk like a white cattle bird
on legs like sticks, with sticking to the Path
between the canes on a district road at dusk.
Playing the Elder. There are no more elders.
Is only old people.

My friends spit on the government.
I do not think is just the government.
Suppose all the gods too old,
suppose they dead and they burning them,
supposing when some cane cutter
start chopping up snakes with a cutlass
he is severing the snake-armed god,
and suppose some hunter has caught
Hanuman in his mischief in a monkey cage.
Suppose all the gods were killed by electric light?

Sunset, a bonfire, roars in my ears;
embers of blown swallows dart and cry,
like women distracted,
around its cremation.
I ascend to my bed of sweet sandalwood.

FOREST OF EUROPE

[*for Joseph Brodsky*]

The last leaves fell like notes from a piano
and left their ovals echoing in the ear;
with gawky music stands, the winter forest
looks like an empty orchestra, its lines
ruled on these scattered manuscripts of snow.

The inlaid copper laurel of an oak
shines through the brown-bricked glass above your head
as bright as whisky, while the wintry breath
of lines from Mandelstam, which you recite,
uncoils as visibly as cigarette smoke.

"The rustling of ruble notes by the lemon Neva."
Under your exile's tongue, crisp under heel,
the gutturals crackle like decaying leaves,
the phrase from Mandelstam circles with light
in a brown room, in barren Oklahoma.

There is a Gulag Archipelago
under this ice, where the salt, mineral spring
of the long Trail of Tears runnels these plains
as hard and open as a herdsman's face
sun-cracked and stubbled with unshaven snow.

Growing in whispers from the Writers' Congress,
the snow circles like Cossacks round the corpse
of a tired Choctaw till it is a blizzard
of treaties and white papers as we lose
sight of the single human through the cause.

So every spring these branches load their shelves,
like libraries with newly published leaves,
till waste recycles them—paper to snow—

but, at zero of suffering, one mind
lasts like this oak with a few brazen leaves.

As the train passed the forest's tortured icons,
the floes clanging like freight yards, then the spires
of frozen tears, the station's screeching steam,
he drew them in a single winter's breath
whose freezing consonants turned into stones.

He saw the poetry in forlorn stations
under clouds vast as Asia, through districts
that could gulp Oklahoma like a grape,
not these tree-shaded prairie halts but space
so desolate it mocked destinations.

Who is that dark child on the parapets
of Europe, watching the evening river mint
its sovereigns stamped with power, not with poets,
the Thames and the Neva rustling like banknotes,
then, black on gold, the Hudson's silhouettes?

From frozen Neva to the Hudson pours,
under the airport domes, the echoing stations,
the tributary of emigrants whom exile
has made as classless as the common cold,
citizens of a language that is now yours,

and every February, every "last autumn,"
you write far from the threshing harvesters
folding wheat like a girl plaiting her hair,
far from Russia's canals quivering with sunstroke,
a man living with English in one room.

The tourist archipelagoes of my South
are prisons too, corruptible, and though
there is no harder prison than writing verse,
what's poetry, if it is worth its salt,
but a phrase men can pass from hand to mouth?

From hand to mouth, across the centuries,
the bread that lasts when systems have decayed,
when, in his forest of barbed-wire branches,
a prisoner circles, chewing the one phrase
whose music will last longer than the leaves,

whose condensation is the marble sweat
of angels' foreheads, which will never dry
till Borealis shuts the peacock lights
of its slow fan from L.A. to Archangel,
and memory needs nothing to repeat.

Frightened and starved, with divine fever
Osip Mandelstam shook, and every
metaphor shuddered him with ague,
each vowel heavier than a boundary stone,
"to the rustling of ruble notes by the lemon Neva,"

but now that fever is a fire whose glow
warms our hands, Joseph, as we grunt like primates
exchanging gutturals in this winter cave
of a brown cottage, while in drifts outside
mastodons force their systems through the snow.

From

THE FORTUNATE TRAVELLER

(1 9 8 1)

PIANO PRACTICE

[*for Mark Strand*]

April, in another fortnight, metropolitan April.
A drizzle glazes the museum's entrance,
like their eyes when they leave you, equivocating spring!
The sun dries the avenue's pumice façade
delicately as a girl tamps tissue on her cheek;
the asphalt shines like a silk hat,
the fountains trot like percherons round the Met,
clip, clop, clip, clop in Belle Epoque Manhattan,
as gutters part their lips to the spring rain—
down avenues hazy as Impressionist clichés,
their gargoyle cornices,
their concrete flowers on chipped pediments,
their subway stops in Byzantine mosaic—
the soul sneezes and one tries to compile
the collage of a closing century,
the epistolary pathos, the old Laforguean ache.

Deserted plazas swept by gusts of remorse,
rain-polished cobbles where a curtained carriage
trotted around a corner of Europe for the last time,
as the canals folded like concertinas.
Now fever reddens the trouble spots of the globe,
rain drizzles on the white iron chairs in the gardens.
Today is Thursday, Vallejo is dying,
but come, girl, get your raincoat, let's look for life
in some café behind tear-streaked windows,
perhaps the *fin de siècle* isn't really finished,
maybe there's a piano playing it somewhere,
as the bulbs burn through the heart of the afternoon
in the season of tulips and the pale assassin.
I called the Muse, she pleaded a headache,
but maybe she was just shy at being seen
with someone who has only one climate,

so I passed the flowers in stone, the sylvan pediments,
alone. It wasn't I who shot the archduke,
I excuse myself of all crimes of that ilk,
muttering the subway's obscene graffiti;
I could offer her nothing but the predictable
pale head-scarf of the twilight's lurid silk.

Well, goodbye, then, I'm sorry I've never gone
to the great city that gave Vallejo fever.
Maybe the Seine outshines the East River,
maybe, but near the Metropolitan
a steel tenor pan
dazzlingly practises something from old Vienna,
the scales skittering like minnows across the sea.

EUROPA

The full moon is so fierce that I can count the
coconuts' cross-hatched shade on bungalows,
their white walls raging with insomnia.
The stars leak drop by drop on the tin plates
of the sea-almonds, and the jeering clouds
are luminously rumpled as the sheets.
The surf, insatiably promiscuous,
groans through the walls; I feel my mind
whiten to moonlight, altering that form
which daylight unambiguously designed,
from a tree to a girl's body bent in foam;
then, treading close, the black hump of a hill,
its nostrils softly snorting, nearing the
naked girl splashing her breasts with silver.
Both would have kept their proper distance still,
if the chaste moon hadn't swiftly drawn the drapes
of a dark cloud, coupling their shapes.

She teases with those flashes, yes, but once
you yield to human horniness, you see
through all that moonshine what they really were,
those gods as seed-bulls, gods as rutting swans—
an overheated farmhand's literature.
Who ever saw her pale arms hook his horns,
her thighs clamped tight in their deep-plunging ride,
watched, in the hiss of the exhausted foam,
her white flesh constellate to phosphorus
as in salt darkness beast and woman come?
Nothing is there, just as it always was,
but the foam's wedge to the horizon-light,
then, wire-thin, the studded armature,
like drops still quivering on his matted hide,
the hooves and horn-points anagrammed in stars.

THE SPOILER'S RETURN

[*for Earl Lovelace*]

I sit high on this bridge in Laventille,
watching that city where I left no will
but my own conscience and rum-eaten wit,
and limers passing see me where I sit,
ghost in brown gabardine, bones in a sack,
and bawl: "Ay, Spoiler, boy! When you come back?"
And those who bold don't feel they out of place
to peel my limeskin back, and see a face
with eyes as cold as a dead macajuel,
and if they still can talk, I answer: "Hell."
I have a room there where I keep a crown,
and Satan send me to check out this town.
Down there, that Hot Boy have a stereo
where, whole day, he does blast my caiso;
I beg him two weeks' leave and he send me
back up, not as no bedbug or no flea,
but in this limeskin hat and floccy suit,
to sing what I did always sing: the truth.
Tell Desperadoes when you reach the hill,
I decompose, but I composing still:

I going to bite them young ladies, partner,
like a hot dog or a hamburger
and if you thin, don't be in a fright
is only big fat women I going to bite.

The shark, racing the shadow of the shark
across clear coral rocks, does make them dark—
that is my premonition of the scene
of what passing over this Caribbean.
Is crab climbing crab-back, in a crab-quarrel,
and going round and round in the same barrel,
is sharks with shirt-jacs, sharks with well-pressed fins,

ripping we small-fry off with razor grins;
nothing ain't change but colour and attire,
so back me up, Old Brigade of Satire,
back me up, Martial, Juvenal, and Pope
(to hang theirself I giving plenty rope),
join Spoiler' chorus, sing the song with me,
Lord Rochester, who praised the nimble flea:

Were I, who to my cost already am
One of those strange, prodigious creatures, Man,
A spirit free, to choose for my own share,
What case of flesh and blood I pleased to wear,
I hope when I die, after burial,
To come back as an insect or animal.

I see these islands and I feel to bawl,
"area of darkness" with V. S. Nightfall.

Lock off your tears, you casting pearls of grief
on a duck's back, a waxen dasheen leaf,
the slime crab's carapace is waterproof
and those with hearing aids turn off the truth,
and their dark glasses let you criticize
your own presumptuous image in their eyes.
Behind dark glasses is just hollow skull,
and black still poor, though black is beautiful.
So, crown and mitre me Bedbug the First—
the gift of mockery with which I'm cursed
is just a insect biting Fame behind,
a vermin swimming in a glass of wine,
that, dipped out with a finger, bound to bite
its saving host, ungrateful parasite,
whose sting, between the cleft arse and its seat,
reminds Authority man is just meat,
a moralist as mordant as the louse
that the good husband brings from the whorehouse,
the flea whose itch to make all Power wince,
will crash a fête, even at his life's expense,

and these pile up in lime pits by the heap,
daily, that our deliverers may sleep.
All those who promise free and just debate,
then blow up radicals to save the state,
who allow, in democracy's defence,
a parliament of spiked heads on a fence,
all you go bawl out, "Spoils, things ain't so bad."
This ain't the Dark Age, is just Trinidad,
is human nature, Spoiler, after all,
it ain't big genocide, is just bohbohl;
safe and conservative, 'fraid to take side,
they say that Rodney commit suicide,
is the same voices that, in the slave ship,
smile at their brothers, "Boy, is just the whip,"
I free and easy, you see me have chain?
A little censorship can't cause no pain,
a little graft can't rot the human mind,
what sweet in goat-mouth sour in his behind.
So I sing with Attila, I sing with Commander,
what right in Guyana, right in Uganda.
The time could come, it can't be very long,
when they will jail calypso for picong,
for first comes television, then the press,
all in the name of Civic Righteousness;
it has been done before, all Power has
made the sky shit and maggots of the stars,
over these Romans lying on their backs,
the hookers swaying their enormous sacks,
until all language stinks, and the truth lies,
a mass for maggots and a fête for flies;
and, for a spineless thing, rumour can twist
into a style the local journalist—
as bland as a green coconut, his manner
routinely tart, his sources the Savannah
and all pretensions to a native art
reduced to giggles at the coconut cart,
where heads with reputations, in one slice,
are brought to earth, when they ain't eating nice;

and as for local Art, so it does go,
the audience have more talent than the show.

Is Carnival, straight Carnival that's all,
the beat is base, the melody bohbohl,
all Port of Spain is a twelve-thirty show,
some playing Kojak, some Fidel Castro,
some Rastamen, but, with or without locks,
to Spoiler is the same old khaki socks,
all Frederick Street stinking like a closed drain,
Hell is a city much like Port of Spain,
what the rain rots, the sun ripens some more,
all in due process and within the law,
as, like a sailor on a spending spree,
we blow our oil-bloated economy
on projects from here to eternity,
and Lord, the sunlit streets break Spoiler's heart,
to have natural gas and not to give a fart,
to see them line up, pitch-oil tin in hand:
each independent, oil-forsaken island,
like jeering at some scrunter with the blues,
while you lend him some need-a-half-sole shoes,
some begging bold as brass, some coming meeker,
but from Jamaica to poor Dominica
we make them know they begging, every loan
we send them is like blood squeezed out of stone,
and giving gives us back the right to laugh
that we couldn't see we own black people starve,
and, more we give, more we congratulate
we-self on our own self-sufficient state.
In all them project, all them Five-Year Plan,
what happen to the Brotherhood of Man?
Around the time I dead it wasn't so,
we sang the Commonwealth of caiso,
we was in chains, but chains made us unite,
now who have, good for them, and who blight, blight;
my bread is bitterness, my wine is gall,
my chorus is the same: "I want to fall."

Oh, wheel of industry, check out your cogs!
Between the knee-high trash and khaki dogs
Arnold's Phoenician trader reach this far,
selling you half-dead batteries for your car;
the children of Tagore, in funeral shroud,
curry favour and chicken from the crowd;
as for the Creoles, check their house, and look,
you bust your brain before you find a book,
when Spoiler see all this, ain't he must bawl,
"area of darkness," with V. S. Nightfall?
Corbeaux like cardinals line the La Basse
in ecumenical patience while you pass
the Beetham Highway—Guard corruption's stench,
you bald, black justices of the High Bench—
and beyond them the firelit mangrove swamps,
ibises practising for postage stamps,
Lord, let me take a taxi South again
and hear, drumming across Caroni Plain,
the tabla in the Indian half hour
when twilight fills the mud huts of the poor,
to hear the tattered flags of drying corn
rattle a sky from which all the gods gone,
their bleached flags of distress waving to me
from shacks, adrift like rafts on a green sea,
"Things ain't go change, they ain't go change at all,"
to my old chorus: "Lord, I want to bawl."
The poor still poor, whatever arse they catch.
Look south from Laventille, and you can watch
the torn brown patches of the Central Plain
slowly restitched by needles of the rain,
and the frayed earth, criss-crossed like old bagasse,
spring to a cushiony quilt of emerald grass,
and who does sew and sow and patch the land?
The Indian. And whose villages turn sand?
The fishermen doomed to stitching the huge net
of the torn foam from Point to La Fillette.

One thing with hell, at least it organize
in soaring circles, when any man dies
he must pass through them first, that is the style,
Jesus was down here for a little while,
cadaverous Dante, big-guts Rabelais,
all of them wave to Spoiler on their way.
Catch us in Satan tent, next carnival:
Lord Rochester, Quevedo, Juvenal,
Maestro, Martial, Pope, Dryden, Swift, Lord Byron,
the lords of irony, the Duke of Iron,
hotly contending for the monarchy
in couplets or the old re-minor key,
all those who gave earth's pompous carnival
fatigue, and groaned "O God, I feel to fall!"
all those whose anger for the poor on earth
made them weep with a laughter beyond mirth,
names wide as oceans when compared with mine
salted my songs, and gave me their high sign.
All you excuse me, Spoiler was in town;
you pass him straight, so now he gone back down.

EARLY POMPEIAN

[*for Norline*]

> *Ere Babylon was dust,*
> *The Magus Zoroaster, my dead child,*
> *Met his own image walking in the garden,*
> *That apparition, sole of men, he saw.*
> —SHELLEY

I

In the first years, when your hair
was parted severely in the Pompeian style,
you resembled those mosaics
whose round eyes
keep their immortal pinpoints, or were,
in laughing days, black olives on a saucer.

Then, one night, years later,
a flaring torch passed slowly down that wall
and lit them, and it was your turn.
Your girlhood was finished, your sorrows were robing
you with the readiness of woman.

The darkness placed a black shawl around your shoulders,
pointed to a colonnade of torches
like palm trees with their fronds on fire,
pointed out the cold flagstones to the sacrificial basin
where the priest stands with his birth-sword.
You nodded. You began to walk.

Voices stretched out their hands and you stepped from the wall.

Past the lowering eyes of rumours,
Past the unblinking stares of the envious,
as, step by step, it faded

behind you, that portrait
with its plum-parted lips,
the skin of pomegranate,
the forehead's blank, unborn bewilderment.
Now you walked in those heel-hollowed steps
in which all of our mothers before us went.

And they led you, pale as the day-delivered moon,
through the fallen white columns of a hospital
to the volcanic bedrock of mud and screams and fire,

into the lava of the damned birth-blood,
the sacrificial gutters,
to where the eye of the stillborn star showed at the end of your road,
a dying star fighting the viruses
of furious constellations,
through the tangled veins, the vineyard of woman's labour,
to a black ditch under the corpuscles of stars,
where the shrunken grape would be born that would not call you
    mother.

In your noble, flickering gaze there was that which repeated
to the stone you carried
"The hardest times are the noblest, my dead child,"
and the torch passed its flame to your tongue,
your face bronzed in the drenches and fires of your finest sweat.

In their black sockets, the pebbles of your eyes
rattled like dice in the tin cup of the blind Fates.
On the black wings of your screams I watched vultures rise,
the laser-lances of pain splinter on the gods' breastplates.
Your nerve ends screamed like fifes,
your temples repeated a drum,
and your firelit head, in profile, passed other faces
as a funeral ship passes the torch-lit headlands
with its princely freight,
your black hair billowing like dishevelled smoke.

Your eyelids whitened like knuckles gripping
the incomprehensible, vague sills of pain.
The door creaked, groaning open, and in its draft, no, a whirlwind,
the lamp that was struggling with darkness was blown out
by the foul breeze off the amniotic sea.

II

By the black harbour,
the black schooners are tired
of going anywhere; the sea
is black and salt as the mind of a woman after labour.

Child, wherever you are,
I am still your father;
let your small, dead star
rock in my heart's black salt,
this sacrificial basin where I weep;
you passed from a sleep to a sleep
with no pilot, without a light.

Beautiful, black, and salt-warm is the starry night,
the smell off the sea is your mother,
as is this wind that moves in the leaves of the wharf under the pavement
    light.

I stare into black water by whose hulls
heaven is rocked like a cradle,
except, except for one extinguished star,
and I think of a hand that stretches out from her bedside for nothing,
and then is withdrawn, remembering where you are.

III

I will let the nights pass,
I shall allow the sun to rise,

I shall let it pass like a torch along a wall
on which there is fadingly set,
stone by fading stone,
the face of an astonished girl, her lips, her black hair parted
in the early Pompeian style.

And what can I write for her
but that when we are stoned with pain,
and we shake our heads wildly from side to side,
saying "no more," "no more again," to certain things,
no more faith, no more hope, only charity,
charity gives faith and hope much stronger wings.

IV

As for you, little star,
my lost daughter, you are
bent in the shape forever
of a curled seed sailing the earth,
in the shape of one question, a comma
that knows before us whether death
is another birth.
                          I had no answer
to that tap-tapping under the dome
of the stomach's round coffin.
I could not guess whether you were calling
to be let in, or to be let go
when the door's groaning blaze
seared the grape-skin
frailty of your eyes crying
against our light, and all that is kin
to the light.
You had sailed without any light
your seven months on the amniotic sea.
You never saw your murderer,
your birth and death giver,
but I will see you everywhere,

I will see you in a boneless
sunbeam that strokes the texture
of things—my arm, the pulseless arm
of an armchair, an iron railing, the leaves
of a dusty plant by a closed door,
in the beams of my own eyes in a mirror.
The lives that we must go on with
are also yours. So I go on
down the apartment steps to the hot
streets of July the twenty-second, nineteen
hundred and eighty, in Trinidad,
amazed that trees are still green
around the Savannah, over the Queen's
Park benches, amazed that my feet can carry
the stone of the earth, the heavier stone of the head,
and I pass through shade where a curled
blossom falls from a black, forked branch
to the asphalt, soundlessly. No cry.
You knew neither this world nor the next,
and, as for us, whose hearts must never harden
against ourselves, who sit on a park bench
like any calm man in a public garden
watching the bright traffic,
we can only wonder why a seed should envy
our suffering, to flower, to suffer,
to die. Gloria, Perdita, I christen
you in the shade, on the bench,
with no hope of the resurrection.
Pardon. Pardon the pride I have taken
in a woman's agony.

THE FORTUNATE TRAVELLER

[for Susan Sontag]

And I heard a voice in the midst of the four beasts say,
A measure of wheat for a penny,
and three measures of barley for a penny;
and see thou hurt not the oil and the wine.

– REVELATION 6·6

I

It was in winter. Steeples, spires
congealed like holy candles. Rotting snow
flaked from Europe's ceiling. A compact man,
I crossed the canal in a grey overcoat,
on one lapel a crimson buttonhole
for the cold ecstasy of the assassin.
In the square coffin manacled to my wrist:
small countries pleaded through the mesh of graphs,
in treble-spaced, Xeroxed forms to the World Bank
on which I had scrawled the one word, MERCY;

      I sat on a cold bench
under some skeletal lindens.
Two other gentlemen, black skins gone grey
as their identical, belted overcoats,
crossed the white river.
They spoke the stilted French
of their dark river,
whose hooked worm, multiplying its pale sickle,
could thin the harvest of the winter streets.
"Then we can depend on you to get us those tractors?"
"I gave my word."
"May my country ask you why you are doing this, sir?"
Silence.

"You know if you betray us, you cannot hide?"
A tug. Smoke trailing its dark cry.

At the window in Haiti, I remember
a gecko pressed against the hotel glass,
with white palms, concentrating head.
With a child's hands. Mercy, monsieur. Mercy.
Famine sighs like a scythe
across the field of statistics and the desert
is a moving mouth. In the hold of this earth
10,000,000 shoreless souls are drifting.
Somalia: 765,000, their skeletons will go under the tidal sand.
"We'll meet you in Bristol to conclude the agreement?"
Steeples like tribal lances, through congealing fog
the cries of wounded church bells wrapped in cotton,
grey mist enfolding the conspirator
like a sealed envelope next to its heart.

No one will look up now to see the jet
fade like a weevil through a cloud of flour.
One flies first-class, one is so fortunate.
Like a telescope reversed, the traveller's eye
swiftly screws down the individual sorrow
to an oval nest of antic numerals,
and the iris, interlocking with this globe,
condenses it to zero, then a cloud.
Beetle-black taxi from Heathrow to my flat.
We are roaches,
riddling the state cabinets, entering the dark holes
of power, carapaced in topcoats,
scuttling around columns, signalling for taxis,
with frantic antennae, to other huddles with roaches;
we infect with optimism, and when
the cabinets crack, we are the first
to scuttle, radiating separately
back to Geneva, Bonn, Washington, London.

Under the dripping planes of Hampstead Heath,
I read her letter again, watching the drizzle
disfigure its pleading like mascara. Margo,
I cannot bear to watch the nations cry.
Then the phone: "We will pay you in Bristol."
Days in fetid bedclothes swallowing cold tea,
the phone stifled by the pillow. The telly
a blue storm with soundless snow.
I'd light the gas and see a tiger's tongue.
I was rehearsing the ecstasies of starvation
for what I had to do. *And have not charity.*

I found my pity, desperately researching
the origins of history, from reed-built communes
by sacred lakes, turning with the first sprocketed
water-driven wheels. I smelled imagination
among bestial hides by the gleam of fat,
seeking in all races a common ingenuity.
I envisaged an Africa flooded with such light
as alchemized the first fields of emmer wheat and barley,
when we savages dyed our pale dead with ochre,
and bordered our temples
with the ceremonial vulva of the conch
in the grey epoch of the obsidian adze.
I sowed the Sahara with rippling cereals,
my charity fertilized these aridities.

What was my field? Late sixteenth century.
My field was a dank acre. A Sussex don,
I taught the Jacobean anxieties: *The White Devil.*
Flamineo's torch startles the brooding yews.
The drawn end comes in strides. I loved my Duchess,
the white flame of her soul blown out between
the smoking cypresses. Then I saw children pounce
on green meat with a rat's ferocity.

I called them up and took the train to Bristol,
my blood the Severn's dregs and silver.

On Severn's estuary the pieces flash,
Iscariot's salary, patron saint of spies.
I thought, who cares how many million starve?
Their rising souls will lighten the world's weight
and level its gull-glittering waterline;
we left at sunset down the estuary.

England recedes. The forked white gull
screeches, circling back.
Even the birds are pulled back by their orbit,
even mercy has its magnetic field.
                              Back in the cabin,
I uncap the whisky, the porthole
mists with glaucoma. By the time I'm pissed,
England, England will be
that pale serrated indigo on the sea-line.
"You are so fortunate, you get to see the world—"
Indeed, indeed, sirs, I have seen the world.
Spray splashes the portholes and vision blurs.

Leaning on the hot rail, watching the hot sea,
I saw them far off, kneeling on hot sand
in the pious genuflections of the locust,
as Ponce's armoured knees crush Florida
to the funereal fragrance of white lilies.

II

Now I have come to where the phantoms live,
I have no fear of phantoms, but of the real.
The Sabbath benedictions of the islands.
Treble clef of the snail on the scored leaf,
the Tantum Ergo of black choristers
soars through the organ pipes of coconuts.
Across the dirty beach surpliced with lace,
they pass a brown lagoon behind the priest,
pale and unshaven in his frayed soutane,

into the concrete church at Canaries;
as Albert Schweitzer moves to the harmonium
of morning, and to the pluming chimneys,
the groundswell lifts *Lebensraum, Lebensraum.*

Black faces sprinkled with continual dew—
dew on the speckled croton, dew
on the hard leaf of the knotted plum tree,
dew on the elephant ears of the dasheen.
Through Kurtz's teeth, white skull in elephant grass,
the imperial fiction sings. Sunday
wrinkles downriver from the Heart of Darkness.
The heart of darkness is not Africa.
The heart of darkness is the core of fire
in the white center of the holocaust.
The heart of darkness is the rubber claw
selecting a scalpel in antiseptic light,
the hills of children's shoes outside the chimneys,
the tinkling nickel instruments on the white altar;
Jacob, in his last card, sent me these verses:
"Think of a God who doesn't lose His sleep
if trees burst into tears or glaciers weep.
So, aping His indifference, I write now,
not Anno Domini: After Dachau."

III

The night maid brings a lamp and draws the blinds.
I stay out on the verandah with the stars.
Breakfast congealed to supper on its plate.

There is no sea as restless as my mind.
The promontories snore. They snore like whales.
Cetus, the whale, was Christ.
The ember dies, the sky smokes like an ash heap.
Reeds wash their hands of guilt and the lagoon
is stained. Louder, since it rained,

a gauze of sandflies hisses from the marsh.
Since God is dead, and these are not His stars,
but man-lit, sulphurous, sanctuary lamps,
it's in the heart of darkness of this earth
that backward tribes keep vigil of His Body,
in deya, lampion, and this bedside lamp.
Keep the news from their blissful ignorance.
Like lice, like lice, the hungry of this earth
swarm to the tree of life. If those who starve
like these rain-flies who shed glazed wings in light
grew from sharp shoulder blades their brittle vans
and soared towards that tree, how it would seethe—
ah, Justice! But fires
drench them like vermin, quotas
prevent them, and they remain
compassionate fodder for the travel book,
its paragraphs like windows from a train,
for everywhere that earth shows its rib cage
and the moon goggles with the eyes of children,
we turn away to read. Rimbaud learned that.
                            Rimbaud, at dusk,
idling his wrist in water past temples
the plumed dates still protect in Roman file,
knew that we cared less for one human face
than for the scrolls in Alexandria's ashes,
that the bright water could not dye his hand
any more than poetry. The dhow's silhouette
moved through the blinding coinage of the river
that, endlessly, until we pay one debt,
shrouds, every night, an ordinary secret.

IV

The drawn sword comes in strides.
It stretches for the length of the empty beach;
the fishermen's huts shut their eyes tight.
A frisson shakes the palm trees,

and sweats on the traveller's tree.
They've found out my sanctuary. Philippe, last night:
"It had two gentlemen in the village yesterday, sir,
asking for you while you was in town.
I tell them you was in town. They send to tell you,
there is no hurry. They will be coming back."

In loaves of cloud, *and have not charity*,
the weevil will make a sahara of Kansas,
the ant shall eat Russia.
Their soft teeth shall make, *and have not charity*,
the harvest's desolation,
and the brown globe crack like a begging bowl,
and though you fire oceans of surplus grain,
and have not charity,

still, through thin stalks,
the smoking stubble, stalks
grasshopper: third horseman,
the leather-helmed locust.

Then all the nations of birds lifted together
the huge net of the shadows of this earth
in multitudinous dialects, twittering tongues,
stitching and crossing it. They lifted up
the shadows of long pines down trackless slopes,
the shadows of glass-faced towers down evening streets,
the shadow of a frail plant on a city sill—
the net rising soundless as night, the birds' cries soundless, until
there was no longer dusk, or season, decline, or weather,
only this passage of phantasmal light
that not the narrowest shadow dared to sever.

And men could not see, looking up, what the wild geese drew,
what the ospreys trailed behind them in silvery ropes
that flashed in the icy sunlight; they could not hear
battalions of starlings waging peaceful cries,
bearing the net higher, covering this world
like the vines of an orchard, or a mother drawing
the trembling gauze over the trembling eyes
of a child fluttering to sleep;
                                        it was the light
that you will see at evening on the side of a hill
in yellow October, and no one hearing knew
what change had brought into the raven's cawing,
the killdeer's screech, the ember-circling chough
such an immense, soundless, and high concern
for the fields and cities where the birds belong,
except it was their seasonal passing, Love,
made seasonless, or, from the high privilege of their birth,
something brighter than pity for the wingless ones
below them who shared dark holes in windows and in houses,

and higher they lifted the net with soundless voices
above all change, betrayals of falling suns,
and this season lasted one moment, like the pause
between dusk and darkness, between fury and peace,
but, for such as our earth is now, it lasted long.

From

MIDSUMMER

(1 9 8 4)

I

The jet bores like a silverfish through volumes of cloud—
clouds that will keep no record of where we have passed,
nor the sea's mirror, nor the coral busy with its own
culture; they aren't doors of dissolving stone,
but pages in a damp culture that come apart.
So a hole in their parchment opens, and suddenly, in a vast
dereliction of sunlight, there's that island known
to the traveller Trollope, and the fellow traveller Froude,
for making nothing. Not even a people. The jet's shadow
ripples over green jungles as steadily as a minnow
through seaweed. Our sunlight is shared by Rome
and your white paper, Joseph. Here, as everywhere else,
it is the same age. In cities, in settlements of mud,
light has never had epochs. Near the rusty harbour
around Port of Spain bright suburbs fade into words—
Maraval, Diego Martin—the highways long as regrets,
and steeples so tiny you couldn't hear their bells,
nor the sharp exclamations of whitewashed minarets
from green villages. The lowering window resounds
over pages of earth, the cane-fields set in stanzas.
Skimming over an ochre swamp like a fast cloud of egrets
are nouns that find their branches as simply as birds.
It comes too fast, this shelving sense of home—
canes rushing the wing, a fence; a world that still stands as
the trundling tires keep shaking and shaking the heart.

Companion in Rome, whom Rome makes as old as Rome,
old as that peeling fresco whose flaking paint
is the clouds, you are crouched in some ancient pensione
where the only new thing is paper, like young St. Jerome
with his rock vault. Tonsured, you're muttering a line
that your exiled country will soon learn by heart,
to a flaking, sunlit ledge where a pigeon gurgles.
Midsummer's furnace casts everything in bronze.
Traffic flows in slow coils, like the doors of a baptistry,
and even the kitten's eyes blaze with Byzantine icons.
That old woman in black, unwrinkling your sheet with a palm,
her home is Rome, its history is her house.
Every Caesar's life has shrunk to a candle's column
in her saucer. Salt cleans their bloodstained togas.
She stacks up the popes like towels in cathedral drawers;
now in her stone kitchen, under the domes of onions,
she slices a light, as thick as cheese, into epochs.
Her kitchen wall flakes like an atlas where, once,
Ibi dracones was written, where unchristened cannibals
gnawed on the dry heads of coconuts as Ugolino did.
Hell's hearth is as cold as Pompeii's. We're punished by bells
as gentle as lilies. Luck to your Roman elegies
that the honey of time will riddle like those of Ovid.
Corals up to their windows in sand are my sacred domes,
gulls circling a seine are the pigeons of my St. Mark's,
silver legions of mackerel race through our catacombs.

Midsummer stretches beside me with its cat's yawn.
Trees with dust on their lips, cars melting down
in its furnace. Heat staggers the drifting mongrels.
The capitol has been repainted rose, the rails
round Woodford Square the color of rusting blood.
Casa Rosada, the Argentinian mood,
croons from the balcony. Monotonous lurid bushes
brush the damp clouds with the ideograms of buzzards
over the Chinese groceries. The oven alleys stifle.
In Belmont, mournful tailors peer over old machines,
stitching June and July together seamlessly.
And one waits for midsummer lightning as the armed sentry
in boredom waits for the crack of a rifle.
But I feed on its dust, its ordinariness,
on the faith that fills its exiles with horror,
on the hills at dusk with their dusty orange lights,
even on the pilot light in the reeking harbour
that turns like a police car's. The terror
is local, at least. Like the magnolia's whorish whiff.
All night, the barks of a revolution crying wolf.
The moon shines like a lost button.
The yellow sodium lights on the wharf come on.
In streets, dishes clatter behind dim windows.
The night is companionable, the future as fierce as
tomorrow's sun everywhere. I can understand
Borges's blind love for Buenos Aires,
how a man feels the streets of a city swell in his hand.

A wind-scraped headland, a sludgy, dishwater sea,
another storm-darkened village with fences of crucified tin.
Give it up to a goat in the rain, whose iron muzzle
can take anything, or to those hopping buzzards
trailing their torn umbrellas in a silvery drizzle
that slimes everything; on the horizon,
the sea's silver language shines like another era,
and, seasick of poverty, my mind is out there.
A storm has wrecked the island, the beach is a mess,
a bent man, crouching, crosses it, cuffed by the wind;
from that gap of blue, with seraphic highmindedness,
the frigate birds are crying that foul weather lifts the soul,
that the sodden red rag of the heart, when it has dried,
will flutter like a lifeguard's flag from its rusty pole.
Though I curse the recurrence of each shining omen,
the sun will come out, and warm up my right hand
like that old crab flexing its fingers outside its hole.
Frail from damp holes, the courageous, pale bestiary
of the sand seethes, the goat nuzzles, head bent
among flashing tins, and the light's flood tide
stutters up to a sandbar in the estuary,
where, making the most of its Egyptian moment,
the heron halts its abrupt, exalted stride—
then a slow frieze of sunlit pelicans.

Since all of your work was really an effort to appease
the past, a need to be admitted among your peers,
let the inheritors question the sibyl and the Sphinx,
and learn that a raceless critic is a primate's dream.
You were distressed by your habitat, you shall not find peace
till you and your origins reconcile; your jaw must droop
and your knuckles scrape the ground of your native place.
Squat on a damp rock round which white lilies stiffen,
pricking their ears; count as the syllables drop
like dew from primeval ferns; note how the earth drinks
language as precious, depending upon the race.
Then, on dank ground, using a twig for a pen,
write Genesis and watch the Word begin.
Elephants will mill at their water hole to trumpet a
new style. Mongoose, arrested in rut,
and saucer-eyed mandrills, drinking from the leaves,
will nod as a dew-lapped lizard discourses on "Lives
of the Black Poets," gripping a branch like a lectern for better
delivery. Already, up in that simian Academe,
a chimp in bifocals, his lower lip a jut,
tears misting the lenses, is turning your *Oeuvres Complètes*.

There was one Syrian, with his bicycle, in our town.
I didn't know if he was a Syrian or an Assyrian.
When I asked him his race, about which Saroyan had written
that all that was left were seventy thousand Assyrians,
where were sixty-nine thousand nine hundred and ninety-nine?
he didn't answer, but smiled at the length of our street.
His pupils flashed like the hot spokes of a chariot,
or the silver wires of his secondhand machine.
I should have asked him about the patterns of birds
migrating in Aramaic, or the correct
pronunciation of wrinkled rivers like "Tagus."
Assyria was far as the ancient world that was taught us,
but then, so was he, from his hot-skinned camels and tents.
I was young and direct and my tense
was the present; if I, in my ignorance,
had distorted time, it was less than some tyrant's
indifference that altered his future.
He wore a white shirt. A black hat. His bicycle
had an iron basket in front. It moved through the mirage
of sugar-cane fields, crediting suits to the cutters.
Next, two more Syrians appeared. All three shared a store
behind which they slept. After that, there was
a sign with that name, so comical to us, of mythical
spade-bearded, anointed, and ringleted kings: ABDUL.
But to me there were still only seventy thousand
Assyrians, and all of them lived next door
in a hot dark room, muttering a language whose sound
had winged lions in it, and birds cut into a wall.

The midsummer sea, the hot pitch road, this grass, these shacks that
    made me,
jungle and razor grass shimmering by the roadside, the edge of art;
wood lice are humming in the sacred wood,
nothing can burn them out, they are in the blood;
their rose mouths, like cherubs, sing of the slow science
of dying—all heads, with, at each ear, a gauzy wing.
Up at Forest Reserve, before branches break into sea,
I looked through the moving, grassed window and thought "pines,"
or conifers of some sort. I thought, they must suffer
in this tropical heat with their child's idea of Russia.
Then suddenly, from their rotting logs, distracting signs
of the faith I betrayed, or the faith that betrayed me—
yellow butterflies rising on the road to Valencia
stuttering "yes" to the resurrection; "yes, yes is our answer,"
the gold-robed Nunc Dimittis of their certain choir.
Where's my child's hymnbook, the poems edged in gold leaf,
the heaven I worship with no faith in heaven,
as the Word turned towards poetry in its grief?
Ah, bread of life, that only love can leaven!
Ah, Joseph, though no man ever dies in his own country,
the grateful grass will grow thick from his heart.

From

THE ARKANSAS TESTAMENT

(1 9 8 7)

SAINT LUCIA'S FIRST COMMUNION

At dusk, on the edge of the asphalt's worn-out ribbon,
in white cotton frock, cotton stockings, a black child stands.
First her, then a small field of her. Ah, it's First Communion!
They hold pink ribboned missals in their hands,

the stiff plaits pinned with their white satin moths.
The caterpillar's accordion, still pumping out the myth
along twigs of cotton from whose parted mouths
the wafer pods in belief without an "if"!

So, all across Saint Lucia thousands of innocents
were arranged on church steps, facing the sun's lens,
erect as candles between squinting parents,
before darkness came on like their blinded saint's.

But if it were possible to pull up on the verge
of the dimming asphalt, before its headlights lance
their eyes, to house each child in my hands,
to lower the window a crack, and delicately urge

the last moth delicately in, I'd let the dark car
enclose their blizzard, and on some black hill,
their pulsing wings undusted, loose them in thousands to stagger
heavenward before it came on: the prejudice, the evil!

THE LIGHT OF THE WORLD

Kaya now, got to have kaya now,
Got to have kaya now,
For the rain is falling.
                    —BOB MARLEY

Marley was rocking on the transport's stereo
and the beauty was humming the choruses quietly.
I could see where the lights on the planes of her cheek
streaked and defined them; if this were a portrait
you'd leave the highlights for last, these lights
silkened her black skin; I'd have put in an earring,
something simple, in good gold, for contrast, but she
wore no jewelry. I imagined a powerful and sweet
odour coming from her, as from a still panther,
and the head was nothing else but heraldic.
When she looked at me, then away from me politely
because any staring at strangers is impolite,
it was like a statue, like a black Delacroix's
Liberty Leading the People, the gently bulging
whites of her eyes, the carved ebony mouth,
the heft of the torso solid, and a woman's,
but gradually even that was going in the dusk,
except the line of her profile, and the highlit cheek,
and I thought, O Beauty, you are the light of the world!

It was not the only time I would think of that phrase
in the sixteen-seater transport that hummed between
Gros Islet and the Market, with its grit of charcoal
and the litter of vegetables after Saturday's sales,
and the roaring rum-shops, outside whose bright doors
you saw drunk women on pavements, the saddest of all things,
winding up their week, winding down their week.
The Market, as it closed on this Saturday night,
remembered a childhood of wandering gas lanterns
hung on poles at street corners, and the old roar

of vendors and traffic, when the lamplighter climbed,
hooked the lantern on its pole, and moved on to another,
and the children turned their faces to its moth, their
eyes white as their nighties; the Market
itself was closed in its involved darkness
and the shadows quarrelled for bread in the shops,
or quarrelled for the formal custom of quarrelling
in the electric rum-shops. I remember the shadows.

The van was slowly filling in the darkening depot.
I sat in the front seat, I had no need for time.
I looked at two girls, one in a yellow bodice
and yellow shorts, with a flower in her hair,
and lusted in peace, the other less interesting.
That evening I had walked the streets of the town
where I was born and grew up, thinking of my mother
with her white hair tinted by the dyeing dusk,
and the tilting box houses that seemed perverse
in their cramp; I had peered into parlours
with half-closed jalousies, at the dim furniture,
Morris chairs, a centre table with wax flowers,
and the lithograph of *Christ of the Sacred Heart*,
vendors still selling to the empty streets—
sweets, nuts, sodden chocolates, nut cakes, mints.

An old woman with a straw hat over her headkerchief
hobbled towards us with a basket; somewhere,
some distance off, was a heavier basket
that she couldn't carry. She was in a panic.
She said to the driver: *"Pas quittez moi à terre,"*
which is, in her patois: "Don't leave me stranded,"
which is, in her history and that of her people:
"Don't leave me on earth," or, by a shift of stress:
"Don't leave me the earth" [for an inheritance];
"Pas quittez moi à terre, Heavenly transport,
Don't leave me on earth, I've had enough of it."
The bus filled in the dark with heavy shadows
that would not be left on earth; no, that would be left

on the earth, and would have to make out.
Abandonment was something they had grown used to.

And I had abandoned them, I knew that there
sitting in the transport, in the sea-quiet dusk,
with men hunched in canoes, and the orange lights
from the Vigie headland, black boats on the water;
I, who could never solidify my shadow
to be one of their shadows, had left them their earth,
their white rum quarrels, and their coal bags,
their hatred of corporals, of all authority.
I was deeply in love with the woman by the window.
I wanted to be going home with her this evening.
I wanted her to have the key to our small house
by the beach at Gros Islet; I wanted her to change
into a smooth white nightie that would pour like water
over the black rocks of her breasts, to lie
simply beside her by the ring of a brass lamp
with a kerosene wick, and tell her in silence
that her hair was like a hill forest at night,
that a trickle of rivers was in her armpits,
that I would buy her Benin if she wanted it,
and never leave her on earth. But the others, too.

Because I felt a great love that could bring me to tears,
and a pity that prickled my eyes like a nettle,
I was afraid I might suddenly start sobbing
on the public transport with the Marley going,
and a small boy peering over the shoulders
of the driver and me at the lights coming,
at the rush of the road in the country darkness,
with lamps in the houses on the small hills,
and thickets of stars; I had abandoned them,
I had left them on earth, I left them to sing
Marley's songs of a sadness as real as the smell
of rain on dry earth, or the smell of damp sand,
and the bus felt warm with their neighbourliness,
their consideration, and the polite partings

in the light of its headlamps. In the blare,
in the thud-sobbing music, the claiming scent
that came from their bodies. I wanted the transport
to continue forever, for no one to descend
and say a good night in the beams of the lamps
and take the crooked path up to the lit door,
guided by fireflies; I wanted her beauty
to come into the warmth of considerate wood,
to the relieved rattling of enamel plates
in the kitchen, and the tree in the yard,
but I came to my stop. Outside the Halcyon Hotel.
The lounge would be full of transients like myself.
Then I would walk with the surf up the beach.
I got off the van without saying good night.
Good night would be full of inexpressible love.
They went on in their transport, they left me on earth.

Then, a few yards ahead, the van stopped. A man
shouted my name from the transport window.
I walked up towards him. He held out something.
A pack of cigarettes had dropped from my pocket.
He gave it to me. I turned, hiding my tears.
There was nothing they wanted, nothing I could give them
but this thing I have called "The Light of the World."

NIGHT FISHING

Line, trawl for each word
with the homesick toss
of a black pirogue anchored
in stuttering phosphorus.

The crab-fishers' torches
keep to the surf's crooked line,
and a cloud's page scorches
with a smell of kerosene.

Thorny stars halo
the sybil's black cry:
"Apothenein thelo
I am longing to die."

But, line, live in the sounds
that ignorant shallows use;
then throw the silvery nouns
to open-mouthed canoes.

ELSEWHERE

[For Stephen Spender]

Somewhere a white horse gallops with its mane
plunging round a field whose sticks
are ringed with barbed wire, and men
break stones or bind straw into ricks.

Somewhere women tire of the shawled sea's
weeping, for the fishermen's dories
still go out. It is blue as peace.
Somewhere they're tired of torture stories.

That somewhere there was an arrest.
Somewhere there was a small harvest
of bodies in the truck. Soldiers rest
somewhere by a road, or smoke in a forest.

Somewhere there is the conference rage
at an outrage. Somewhere a page
is torn out, and somehow the foliage
no longer looks like leaves but camouflage.

Somewhere there is a comrade,
a writer lying with his eyes wide open
on mattress ticking, who will not read
this, or write. How to make a pen?

And here we are free for a while, but
elsewhere, in one-third, or one-seventh
of this planet, a summary rifle butt
breaks a skull into the idea of a heaven

where nothing is free, where blue air
is paper-frail, and whatever we write
will be stamped twice, a blue letter,
its throat slit by the paper knife of the state.

Through these black bars
hollowed faces stare. Fingers
grip the cross bars of these stanzas
and it is here, because somewhere else

their stares fog into oblivion
thinly, like the faceless numbers
that bewilder you in your telephone
diary. Like last year's massacres.

The world is blameless. The darker crime
is to make a career of conscience,
to feel through our own nerves the silent scream
of winter branches, wonders read as signs.

Are they earlier, these
days without afternoons,
whose lamps like crosiers
ask the same questions?

"Will you laugh on the stair
at my fumbling key?
Will your bedroom mirror
stay all day empty?"

Thunderous traffic
shakes snow from a bridge.
Ice floes crack
from the flaw in marriage.

Wind taps my shoulder
to cross on my sign;
crouched engines shudder
at their starting line.

On the sidewalk's sludge
to our lightless house,
I pass the closed church
and its business hours,

along the burnt aisles
of skeletal trees
with no sign of a cardinal's
fiery surplice;

bursitic fingers
on a white fence contract
and the huge iris goes
grey with cataract,

while before me my wish
runs ahead to each room,
turning switch after switch
on to its own welcome;

one of mufflered shadows
on our street, I walk
past orange windows
where marriages work,

raking a moustache
with a tongue that tastes
not your lips, but ash,
in a cold fireplace,

that sour grey ash
such as birch logs make,
spiking every eyelash
in its neuralgic mask,

as the spreading lichen
multiplies its white cells,
our white block as stricken
as that hospital's,

where our child was lost,
as I watched through glass
the white-sheeted ghosts
of the mothers pass.

Snow climbs higher on
the railings, its drifts
shorten the black iron
spikes into arrowheads;

on Brookline's white prairie,
bent, shaggy forms blow—

heads down, thinning out yearly
like the buffalo

in this second Ice Age
that is promised us
by hot gospellers' rage
or white-smocked scientists,

and, at the last lamp,
before the dun door,
I feel winter's cramp
tighter than before.

Spidery damask
laces the panes; it freezes
until the arching mask
of Tragedy sneezes

on theatre façades in our
comic opera, and plaster
flakes fall on the furniture
of shrouded Boston, and faster

than a mine shaft caving in
I can see the black hole
we have made of heaven.
I scrape each boot sole

on the step. Then stamp
at the ice-welded door.
I cannot break through its clamp
to the fire at earth's core.

I am growing more scared of
your queue of dresses
hanging like questions, the love
of a hairpin pierces

me. The key cannot fit.
Either it has swollen
or the brass shrunk. I fight
the lock. Then I lean,

gasping smoke. Despair
can be wide, it can whiten
the Arctic, but it's clear
as I force the door open

that it's not really the end of
this world, but our own,
that I have had enough
of any love with you gone.

The cold light in the oven
grins again at the news.
I tuck our quilt even.
I lie down in my shoes.

By the bed, brown silt
streaks my old coffee cup.
I forgot to buy salt.
I eat standing up.

My faith lost in answers,
apples, firelight, bread,
in windows whose branches
left you cold, and bored.

FOR ADRIAN

APRIL 14, 1986

[*To Grace, Ben, Judy, Junior, Norline, Katryn, Gem, Stanley, and Diana*]

Look, and you will see that the furniture is fading,
that a wardrobe is as insubstantial as a sunset,

that I can see through you, the tissue of your leaves,
the light behind your veins; why do you keep sobbing?

The days run through the light's fingers like dust
or a child's in a sandpit. When you see the stars

do you burst into tears? When you look at the sea
isn't your heart full? Do you think your shadow

can be as long as the desert? I am a child, listen,
I did not invite or invent angels. It is easy

to be an angel, to speak now beyond my eight years,
to have more vestal authority, and to know,

because I have now entered a wisdom, not a silence.
Why do you miss me? I am not missing you, sisters,

neither Judith, whose hair will banner like the leopard's
in the pride of her young bearing, nor Katryn, not Gem

sitting in a corner of her pain, nor my aunt, the one
with the soft eyes that have soothed the one who writes this,

I would not break your heart, and you should know it;
I would not make you suffer, and you should know it;

and I am not suffering, but it is hard to know it.
I am wiser, I share the secret that is only a silence,

with the tyrants of the earth, with the man who piles rags
in a creaking cart, and goes around a corner

of a square at dusk. You measure my age wrongly,
I am not young now, nor old, not a child, nor a bud

snipped before it flowered, I am part of the muscle
of a galloping lion, or a bird keeping low over

dark canes; and what, in your sorrow, in our faces
howling like statues, you call a goodbye

is—I wish you would listen to me—a different welcome,
which you will share with me, and see that it is true.

All this the child spoke inside me, so I wrote it down.
As if his closing grave were the smile of the earth.

THE ARKANSAS TESTAMENT

[*For Michael Harper*]

I

Over Fayetteville, Arkansas,
a slope of memorial pines
guards the stone slabs of forces
fallen for the Confederacy
at some point in the Civil War.
The young stones, flat on their backs,
their beards curling like mosses,
have no names; an occasional surge
in the pines mutters their roster
while their centennial siege,
their entrenched metamorphosis
into cones and needles, goes on.
Over Arkansas, they can see
between the swaying cracks
in the pines the blue of the Union,
as the trunks get rustier.

II

It was midwinter. The dusk was
yielding in flashes of metal
from a slowly surrendering sun
on the billboards, storefronts, and signs
along Highway 71,
then on the brass-numbered doors
of my $17.50 motel,
and the slab of my cold key.
Jet-lagged and travel-gritty,
I fell back on the double bed
like Saul under neighing horses

on the highway to Damascus,
and lay still, as Saul does,
till my name re-entered me,
and felt, through the chained door,
dark entering Arkansas.

III

I stared back at the Celotex
ceiling of room 16,
my coat still on, for minutes
as the key warmed my palm—
TV, telephone, maid service,
and a sense of the parking lot
through cinder blocks—homesick
for islands with fringed shores
like the mustard-gold coverlet.
A roach crossed its oceanic
carpet with scurrying oars
to a South that it knew, calm
shallows of crystalline green.
I studied again how glare
dies on a wall, till a complex
neon scribbled its signature.

IV

At the desk, crouched over Mr. ———
I had felt like changing my name
for one beat at the register.
Instead, I'd kept up the game
of pretending whoever I was,
or am, or will be, are the same:
"How'll you pay for this, sir?
Cash or charge?" I missed the
chance of answering, "In kind,

like my colour." But her gaze
was corn-country, her eyes frayed
denim. "American Express."
On a pennant, with snarling tusk,
a razorback charged. A tress
of loose hair lifted like maize
in the lounge's indigo dusk.

V

I dozed off in the early dark
to a smell of detergent pine
and they faded with me: the rug
with its shag, pine-needled floor,
the without-a-calendar wall
now hung with the neon's sign,
no thin-lipped Gideon Bible,
no bed lamp, no magazine,
no bristle-faced fiddler
sawing at "Little Brown Jug,"
or some brochure with a landmark
by which you know Arkansas,
or a mountain spring's white babble,
nothing on a shelf, no shelves;
just a smudge on a wall, the mark
left by two uncoiling selves.

VI

I crucified my coat on one wire
hanger, undressed for bathing,
then saw that other, full-length,
alarmed in the glass coffin
of the bathroom door. Right there,
I decided to stay unshaven,
unsaved, if I found the strength.

Oh, for a day's dirt, unshowered,
no plug for my grovelling razor,
to reek of the natural coward
I am, to make this a place for
disposable shavers as well
as my own disposable people!
On a ridge over Fayetteville,
higher than any steeple,
is a white-hot electric cross.

VII

It burns the back of my mind.
It scorches the skin of night;
as a candle repeats the moment
of being blown out, it remained
when I switched off the ceiling light.
That night I slept like the dead,
or a drunk in the tank, like moss
on a wall, like a lover happier
in the loss of love, like soldiers
under the pines, but, as I dreaded,
rose too early. It was four.
Maybe five. I only guessed
by the watch I always keep
when my own house is at rest.
I opened the motel door.
The hills never turned in their sleep.

VIII

Pyjamas crammed in my jacket,
the bottoms stuffed into trousers
that sagged, I needed my fix—
my 5 a.m. caffeine addiction.
No rooster crew brassily back at

the white-neon crucifix,
and Arkansas smelt as sweet
as a barn door opening. Like horses
in their starlit, metallic sweat,
parked cars grazed in their stalls.
Dawn was fading the houses
to an even Confederate grey.
On the far side of the highway,
a breeze turned the leaves of an aspen
to the First Epistle of Paul's
to the Corinthians.

IX

The asphalt, quiet as a Sabbath,
by municipal sprinklers anointed,
shot its straight and narrow path
in the white, converging arrows
of Highway 71. They pointed
to Florida, as if tired warriors
dropped them on the Trail of Tears,
but nothing stirred in response
except two rabbinical willows
with nicotine beards, and a plaid
jacket Frisbeeing papers
from a bike to silvery lawns,
tires hissing the peace that passeth
understanding under the black elms,
and morning in Nazareth
was Fayetteville's and Jerusalem's.

X

Hugging walls in my tippler's hop—
the jive of shuffling bums,
a beat that comes from the chain—

I waited for a while by the grass
of a urinous wall to let
the revolving red eye on top
of a cruising police car pass.
In an all-night garage I saw
the gums of a toothless sybil
in garage tires, and she said:
STAY BLACK AND INVISIBLE
TO THE SIRENS OF ARKANSAS.
The snakes coiled on the pumps
hissed with their metal mouths:
Your shadow still hurts the South,
like Lee's slowly reversing sword.

XI

There's nothing to understand
in hunger. I watched the shell
of a white sun tapping its yolk
on the dark crust of Fayetteville,
and hurried up in my walk
past warming brick to the smell
of hash browns. Abounding light
raced towards me like a mongrel
hoping that it would be caressed
by my cold, roughening hand,
and I prayed that all could be blest
down Highway 71, the grey calm
of the lanes where a lion
lies down on its traffic island,
a post chevroning into a palm.
The world warmed to its work.

XII

But two doors down, a cafeteria
reminded me of my race.
A soak cursed his vinyl table
steadily, not looking up.
A tall black cook setting glazed
pies, a beehive-blond waitress,
lips like a burst strawberry,
and her "Mornin' " like maple syrup.
Four DEERE caps talking deer hunting.
I looked for my own area.
The muttering black decanter
had all I needed; it could sigh for
Sherman's smoking march to Atlanta
or the march to Montgomery.
I was still nothing. A cipher
in its bubbling black zeros, here.

XIII

The self-contempt that it takes
to find my place card among any
of the faces reflected in lakes
of lacquered mahogany
comes easily now. I have laughed
loudest until silence kills
the shoptalk. A fork clicks
on its plate; a cough's rifle shot
shivers the chandeliered room.
A bright arm shakes its manacles.
Every candle-struck face stares into
the ethnic abyss. In the oval
of a silver spoon, the window
bent in a wineglass, the offal
of flattery fed to my craft,
I watch the bright clatter resume.

XIV

I bagged the hot Styrofoam coffee
to the recently repealed law
that any black out after curfew
could be shot dead in Arkansas.
Liberty turns its face; the doctrine
of Aryan light is upheld
as sunrise stirs the lion-
coloured grasses of the veld.
Its seam glints in the mind
of the golden Witwatersrand,
whose clouds froth like a beer stein
in the Boer's sunburnt hand;
the world is flushed with fever.
In some plaid-flannel wood
a buck is roped to a fender—
it is something in their blood.

XV

In a world I saw without end as
one highway with signs, low brown
motels, burger haciendas,
a neat, evangelical town
now pointed through decorous oaks
its calendar comfort—scary
with its simple, God-fearing folks.
Evil was as ordinary
here as good. I kept my word.
This, after all, was the South,
whose plough was still the sword,
its red earth dust in the mouth,
whose grey divisions and dates
swirl in the pine-scented air—
wherever the heart hesitates
that is its true frontier.

XVI

On front porches every weak lamp
went out; on the frame windows
day broadened into the prose
of an average mid-American town.
My metre dropped its limp.
Sunlight flooded Arkansas.
Cold sunshine. I had to draw
my coat tight from the cold, or
suffer the nips of arthritis,
the small arrows that come with age;
the sun began to massage
the needles in the hill's shoulder
with its balsam, but hairs
fall on my collar as I write this
in shorter days, darker years,
more hatred, more racial rage.

XVII

The light, being amber, ignored
the red and green traffic stops,
and, since it had never met me,
went past me without a nod.
It sauntered past the shops,
peered into AUTOMOBILE SALES,
where a serenely revolving Saab
sneered at it. At INDIAN CRAFTS
it regilded the Southern Gothic
sign, climbed one of the trails,
touching leaves as it sent
shadows squirrelling. Its shafts,
like the lasers of angels, went
through the pines guarding each slab
of the Confederate Cemetery,
piercing the dead with the quick.

XVIII

Perhaps in these same pines runs,
with cross ties of bleeding thorns,
the track of the Underground Rail-
road way up into Canada,
and what links the Appalachians
is the tinkle of ankle chains
running north, where history is harder
to bear: the hypocrisy
of clouds with Puritan collars.
Wounds from the Indian wars
cut into the soft plank tables
by the picnic lake, and birches
peel like canoes, and the maple's
leaves tumble like Hessians;
hills froth into dogwood, churches
arrow into the Shawmut sky.

XIX

O lakes of pines and still water,
where the wincing muzzles of deer
make rings that widen the idea
of the state past the calendar!
Does this aging Democracy
remember its log-cabin dream,
the way that a man past fifty
imagines a mountain stream?
The pines huddle in quotas
on the lake's calm waterline
that draws across them straight as
the stroke of a fountain pen.
My shadow's scribbled question
on the margin of the street
asks, Will I be a citizen
or an afterthought of the state?

XX

Can I bring a palm to my heart
and sing, with eyes on the pole
whose manuscript banner boasts
of the Union with thirteen stars
crossed out, but is borne by the ghosts
of sheeted hunters who ride
to the fire-white cross of the South?
Can I swear to uphold my art
that I share with them too, or worse,
pretend all is past and curse
from the picket lines of my verse
the concept of Apartheid?
The shadow bends to the will
as our oaths of allegiance bend
to the state. What we know of evil
is that it will never end.

XXI

The original sin is our seed,
and that acorn fans into an oak;
the umbrella of Africa's shade,
despite this democracy's mandates,
still sprouts from a Southern street
that holds grey black men in a stoop,
their flintlock red eyes. We have shared
our passbook's open secret
in the hooded eyes of a cop,
the passerby's unuttered aside,
the gesture involuntary, signs,
the excessively polite remark
that turns an idea to acid
in the gut, and here I felt its
poison infecting the hill pines,
all the way to the top.

XXII

Sir, you urge us to divest
ourselves of all earthly things,
like these camphor cabinets
with their fake-pine coffins;
to empty the drawer of the chest
and look far beyond the hurt
on which a cross looks down,
as light floods this asphalt
car park, like the rush Tower
where Raleigh brushes his shirt
and Villon and his brothers cower
at the shadow of the still knot.
There are things that my craft cannot
wield, and one is power;
and though only old age earns the
right to an abstract noun

XXIII

this, Sir, is my Office,
my Arkansas Testament,
my two cupfuls of Cowardice,
my sure, unshaven Salvation,
my people's predicament.
Bless the increasing bliss
of truck tires over asphalt,
and these stains I cannot remove
from the self-soiled heart. This
noon, some broad-backed maid,
half-Indian perhaps, will smooth
this wheat-coloured double bed,
and afternoon sun will reprint
the bars of a flag whose cloth—
over motel, steeple, and precinct—
must heal the stripes and the scars.

XXIV

I turned on the TV set.
A light, without any noise,
in amber successive stills,
stirred the waves off Narragansett
and the wheat-islanded towns.
I watched its gold bars explode
on the wagon axles of Mormons,
their brows and hunched shoulders set
toward Zion, their wide oxen road
raising dust in the gopher's nostrils;
then a gravelly announcer's voice
was embalming the Black Hills—
it bade the Mojave rejoice,
it switched off the neon rose
of Vegas, and its shafts came to
the huge organ pipes of sequoias,
the Pacific, and *Today*'s news.

From

OMEROS

(1 9 9 0)

CHAPTER I

I

"This is how, one sunrise, we cut down them canoes."
Philoctete smiles for the tourists, who try taking
his soul with their cameras. "Once wind bring the news

to the *laurier-cannelles*, their leaves start shaking
the minute the axe of sunlight hit the cedars,
because they could see the axes in our own eyes.

Wind lift the ferns. They sound like the sea that feed us
fishermen all our life, and the ferns nodded 'Yes,
the trees have to die.' So, fists jam in our jacket,

cause the heights was cold and our breath making feathers
like the mist, we pass the rum. When it came back, it
give us the spirit to turn into murderers.

I lift up the axe and pray for strength in my hands
to wound the first cedar. Dew was filling my eyes,
but I fire one more white rum. Then we advance."

For some extra silver, under a sea-almond,
he shows them a scar made by a rusted anchor,
rolling one trouser-leg up with the rising moan

of a conch. It has puckered like the corolla
of a sea-urchin. He does not explain its cure.
"It have some things"—he smiles—"worth more than a dollar."

He has left it to a garrulous waterfall
to pour out his secret down La Sorcière, since
the tall laurels fell, for the ground-dove's mating call

to pass on its note to the blue, tacit mountains
whose talkative brooks, carrying it to the sea,
turn into idle pools where the clear minnows shoot

and an egret stalks the reeds with one rusted cry
as it stabs and stabs the mud with one lifting foot.
Then silence is sawn in half by a dragonfly

as eels sign their names along the clear bottom-sand,
when the sunrise brightens the river's memory
and waves of huge ferns are nodding to the sea's sound.

Although smoke forgets the earth from which it ascends,
and nettles guard the holes where the laurels were killed,
an iguana hears the axes, clouding each lens

over its lost name, when the hunched island was called
"Iounalao," "Where the iguana is found."
But, taking its own time, the iguana will scale

the rigging of vines in a year, its dewlap fanned,
its elbows akimbo, its deliberate tail
moving with the island. The slit pods of its eyes

ripened in a pause that lasted for centuries,
that rose with the Aruacs' smoke till a new race
unknown to the lizard stood measuring the trees.

These were their pillars that fell, leaving a blue space
for a single God where the old gods stood before.
The first god was a gommier. The generator

began with a whine, and a shark, with sidewise jaw,
sent the chips flying like mackerel over water
into trembling weeds. Now they cut off the saw,

still hot and shaking, to examine the wound it
had made. They scraped off its gangrenous moss, then ripped
the wound clear of the net of vines that still bound it

to this earth, and nodded. The generator whipped
back to its work, and the chips flew much faster as
the shark's teeth gnawed evenly. They covered their eyes

from the splintering nest. Now, over the pastures
of bananas, the island lifted its horns. Sunrise
trickled down its valleys, blood splashed on the cedars,

and the grove flooded with the light of sacrifice.
A gommier was cracking. Its leaves an enormous
tarpaulin with the ridgepole gone. The creaking sound

made the fishermen leap back as the angling mast
leant slowly towards the troughs of ferns; then the ground
shuddered under the feet in waves, then the waves passed.

II

Achille looked up at the hole the laurel had left.
He saw the hole silently healing with the foam
of a cloud like a breaker. Then he saw the swift

crossing the cloud-surf, a small thing, far from its home,
confused by the waves of blue hills. A thorn vine gripped
his heel. He tugged it free. Around him, other ships

were shaping from the saw. With his cutlass he made
a swift sign of the cross, his thumb touching his lips
while the height rang with axes. He swayed back the blade,

and hacked the limbs from the dead god, knot after knot,
wrenching the severed veins from the trunk as he prayed:
"Tree! You can be a canoe! Or else you cannot!"

The bearded elders endured the decimation
of their tribe without uttering a syllable
of that language they had uttered as one nation,

the speech taught their saplings: from the towering babble
of the cedar to green vowels of *bois-campêche*.
The *bois-flot* held its tongue with the *laurier-cannelle*,

the red-skinned logwood endured the thorns in its flesh,
while the Aruacs' patois crackled in the smell
of a resinous bonfire that turned the leaves brown

with curling tongues, then ash, and their language was lost.
Like barbarians striding columns they have brought down,
the fishermen shouted. The gods were down at last.

Like pygmies they hacked the trunks of wrinkled giants
for paddles and oars. They were working with the same
concentration as an army of fire-ants.

But vexed by the smoke for defaming their forest,
blow-darts of mosquitoes kept needling Achille's trunk.
He frotted white rum on both forearms that, at least,

those that he flattened to asterisks would die drunk.
They went for his eyes. They circled them with attacks
that made him weep blindly. Then the host retreated

to high bamboo like the archers of Aruacs
running from the muskets of cracking logs, routed
by the fire's banner and the remorseless axe

hacking the branches. The men bound the big logs first
with new hemp and, like ants, trundled them to a cliff
to plunge through tall nettles. The logs gathered that thirst

for the sea which their own vined bodies were born with.
Now the trunks in eagerness to become canoes
ploughed into breakers of bushes, making raw holes

of boulders, feeling not death inside them, but use—
to roof the sea, to be hulls. Then, on the beach, coals
were set in their hollows that were chipped with an adze.

A flat-bed truck had carried their rope-bound bodies.
The charcoals, smouldering, cored the dugouts for days
till heat widened the wood enough for ribbed gunwales.

Under his tapping chisel Achille felt their hollows
exhaling to touch the sea, lunging towards the haze
of bird-printed islets, the beaks of their parted bows.

Then everything fit. The pirogues crouched on the sand
like hounds with sprigs in their teeth. The priest
sprinkled them with a bell, then he made the swift's sign.

When he smiled at Achille's canoe, *In God We Troust*,
Achille said: "Leave it! Is God' spelling and mine."
After Mass one sunrise the canoes entered the troughs

of the surpliced shallows, and their nodding prows
agreed with the waves to forget their lives as trees;
one would serve Hector and another, Achilles.

III

Achille peed in the dark, then bolted the half-door shut.
It was rusted from sea-blast. He hoisted the fishpot
with the crab of one hand; in the hole under the hut

he hid the cinder-block step. As he neared the depot,
the dawn breeze salted him coming up the grey street
past sleep-tight houses, under the sodium bars

of street-lamps, to the dry asphalt scraped by his feet;
he counted the small blue sparks of separate stars.
Banana fronds nodded to the undulating

anger of roosters, their cries screeching like red chalk
drawing hills on a board. Like his teacher, waiting,
the surf kept chafing at his deliberate walk.

By the time they met at the wall of the concrete shed
the morning star had stepped back, hating the odour
of nets and fish-guts; the light was hard overhead

and there was a horizon. He put the net by the door
of the depot, then washed his hands in its basin.
The surf did not raise its voice, even the ribbed hounds

around the canoes were quiet; a flask of l'absinthe
was passed by the fishermen, who made smacking sounds
and shook at the bitter bark from which it was brewed.

This was the light that Achille was happiest in.
When, before their hands gripped the gunwales, they stood
for the sea-width to enter them, feeling their day begin.

CHAPTER III

I

"Touchez-i, encore: N'ai fendre choux-ous-ou, salope!"
"Touch it again, and I'll split your arse, you bitch!"
"Moi j'a dire—'ous pas prêter un rien. 'Ous ni shallope,

'ous ni seine, 'ous croire 'ous ni choeur campêche?"
"I told you, borrow nothing of mine. You have a canoe,
and a net. Who you think you are? Logwood Heart?"

"'Ous croire 'ous c'est roi Gros Îlet? Voleur homme!"
"You think you're king of Gros Islet, you tin-stealer?"
Then in English: "I go show you who is king! Come!"

Hector came out from the shade. And Achille, the
moment he saw him carrying the cutlass, *un homme*
fou, a madman eaten with envy, replaced the tin

he had borrowed from Hector's canoe neatly back in the prow
of Hector's boat. Then Achille, who had had enough
of this madman, wiped and hefted his own blade.

And now the villagers emerged from the green shade
of the almonds and wax-leaved manchineels, for the face-off
that Hector wanted. Achille walked off and waited

at the warm shallows' edge. Hector strode towards him.
The villagers followed, as the surf abated
its sound, its fear cowering at the beach's rim.

Then, far out at sea, in a sparkling shower
arrows of rain arched from the emerald breakwater
of the reef, the shafts travelling with clear power

in the sun, and behind them, ranged for the slaughter,
stood villagers, shouting, with a sound like the shoal,
and hoisting arms to the light. Hector ran, splashing

in shallows mixed with the drizzle, towards Achille,
his cutlass lifted. The surf, in anger, gnashing
its tail like a foaming dogfight. Men can kill

their own brothers in rage, but the madman who tore
Achille's undershirt from one shoulder also tore
at his heart. The rage that he felt against Hector

was shame. To go crazy for an old bailing tin
crusted with rust! The duel of these fishermen
was over a shadow and its name was Helen.

CHAPTER IV

III

I sat on the white terrace waiting for the cheque.
Our waiter, in a black bow tie, plunged through the sand
between the full deck-chairs, bouncing to discotheque

music from the speakers, a tray sailed in one hand.
The tourists revolved, grilling their backs in their noon
barbecue. The waiter was having a hard time

with his leather soles. They kept sliding down a dune,
but his tray teetered without spilling gin-and-lime
on a scorched back. He was determined to meet the

beach's demands, like a Lawrence of St. Lucia,
except that he was trudging towards a litre
of self-conscious champagne. Like any born loser

he soon kicked the bucket. He rested his tray down,
wiped the sand from the ice-cubes, then plunked the cubes in
the bucket, then the bottle; after this was done,

he seemed ready to help the wife stuff her boobs in
her halter, while her husband sat boiling with rage
like a towelled sheik. Then Lawrence frowned at a mirage.

That was when I turned with him towards the village,
and saw, through the caging wires of the noon sky,
a beach with its padding panther; now the mirage

dissolved to a woman with a madras head-tie,
but the head proud, although it was looking for work.
I felt like standing in homage to a beauty

that left, like a ship, widening eyes in its wake.
"Who the hell is that?" a tourist near my table
asked a waitress. The waitress said, "She? She too proud!"

As the carved lids of the unimaginable
ebony mask unwrapped from its cotton-wool cloud,
the waitress sneered, "Helen." And all the rest followed.

CHAPTER V

III

How fast it fades! Maud thought; the enamelled sky,
the gilded palms, the bars like altars of raffia,
even for that Madonna bathing her baby

with his little shrimp thing! One day the Mafia
will spin these islands round like roulette. What use is
Dennis's devotion when their own ministers

cash in on casinos with their old excuses
of more jobs? Their future felt as sinister as
that of that ebony girl in her yellow dress.

"There's our trouble," Maud muttered into her glass. In
a gust that leant the triangular sails of the
surfers, Plunkett saw the pride of Helen passing

in the same yellow frock Maud had altered for her.
"She looks better in it"—Maud smiled—"but the girl lies
so much, and she stole. What'll happen to her life?"

"God knows," said Plunkett, following the butterfly's
yellow-panelled wings that once belonged to his wife,
the black V of the velvet back, near the shallows.

Her head was lowered; she seemed to drift like a waif,
not like the arrogant servant that ruled their house.
It was at that moment that he felt a duty

towards her hopelessness, something to redress
(he punned relentlessly) that desolate beauty
so like her island's. He drained the foaming Guinness.

Seychelles. Seashells. One more. In the olive saucer,
the dry stones were piling up, their green pith sucked dry.
Got what we took from them, yes sir! Quick, because the

Empire was ebbing. He watched the silhouette
of his wife, her fine profile set in an oval
ivory cloud, like a Victorian locket,

as when, under crossed swords, she lifted the lace veil.
The flag then was sliding down from the hill-stations
of the Upper Punjab, like a collapsing sail;

an elephant folded its knees, its striations
wrinkling like the tea-pavilions after the Raj,
whose ebbing surf lifted the coastlines of nations

as lacy as Helen's shift. In the noon's mirage
the golden palms shook their tassels, Eden's Egypt
sank in the tinted sand. The Giza pyramids

darkened with the sharpening Pitons, as Achille shipped
both oars like rifles. Clouds of delivered Muslims
foamed into the caves of mosques, and honour and glory

faded like crested brandies. Then remorseful hymns
soared in the stone-webbed Abbey. *Memento mori*
in the drumbeat of Remembrance Day. Pigeons whirr

over Trafalgar. Helen needed a history,
that was the pity that Plunkett felt towards her.
Not his, but her story. Not theirs, but Helen's war.

The name, with its historic hallucination,
brightened the beach; the butterfly, to Plunkett's joy,
twinkling from myrmidon to myrmidon, from one

sprawled tourist to another. Her village was Troy,
its smoke obscuring soldiers fallen in battle.
Then her unclouding face, her breasts were its Pitons,

the palms' rusted lances swirled in the death-rattle
of the gargling shoal; for her Gaul and Briton
had mounted fort and redoubt, the ruined barracks

with its bushy tunnel and its penile cannon;
for her cedars fell in green sunrise to the axe.
His mind drifted with the smoke of his reverie

out to the channel. Lawrence arrived. He said:
"I changing shift, Major. Major?" Maud tapped his knee.
"Dennis. The bill." But the bill had never been paid.

Not to that housemaid swinging a plastic sandal
by the noon sea, in a dress that she had to steal.
Wars. Wars thin like sea-smoke, but their dead were real.

He smiled at the mythical hallucination
that went with the name's shadow; the island was once
named Helen; its Homeric association

rose like smoke from a siege; the Battle of the Saints
was launched with that sound, from what was the "Gibraltar
of the Caribbean," after thirteen treaties

while she changed prayers often as knees at an altar,
till between French and British her final peace
was signed at Versailles. All of this came to his mind

as Lawrence came staggering up the terrace
with the cheque finally, and that treaty was signed;
the paper was crossed by the shadow of her face

as it was at Versailles, two centuries before,
by the shade of Admiral Rodney's gathering force;
a lion-headed island remembering war,

its crouched flanks tawny with drought, and on its ridge, grass
stirred like its mane. For a while he watched the waiter
move through the white iron shields of the white terrace.

In the village Olympiad, on St. Peter's Day,
he served as official starter with a flare-gun
borrowed from the manager of the marina.

It wasn't Aegean. They climbed no Parthenon
to be laurelled. The depot faced their arena,
the sea's amphitheatre. When one wore a crown—

victor ludorum—no one knew what it meant, or
cared to be told. The Latin syllables would drown
in the clapping dialect of the crowd. Hector

would win, or Achille by a hair; but everyone
knew as the crossing ovals of their thighs would soar
in jumps down the cheering aisle, or their marathon

six times round the village, that the true bounty was
Helen, not a shield nor the ham saved for Christmas;
as one slid down the greased pole to factional roars.

CHAPTER XXIV

I

From his heart's depth he knew she was never coming
back, as he followed the skipping of a sea-swift
over the waves' changing hills, as if the humming

horizon-bow had made Africa the target
of its tiny arrow. When he saw the swift flail
and vanish in a trough he knew he'd lost Helen.

The mate was cleaning the bilge with the rusted pail
when the swift reappeared like a sunlit omen,
widening the joy that had vanished from his work.

Sunlight entered his hands, they gave that skillful twist
that angled the blade for the next stroke. Half-awake
from last night's blocko, the mate waveringly pissed

over the side, keeping his staggering balance.
"Fish go get drunk." Achille grinned. The mate cupped his hands
in the sea and lathered his head. "All right. Work start!"

He fitted the trawling rods. Achille felt the rim
of the brimming morning being brought like a gift
by the handles of the headland. He was at home.

This was his garden. God bless the speed of the swift,
God bless the wet head of the mate sparkling with foam,
and his heart trembled with enormous tenderness

for the purple-blue water and the wilting shore
tight and thin as a fishline, and the hill's blue smoke,
his muscles bulging like porpoises from each oar,

but the wrists wrenched deftly after the lifted stroke,
mesmerizing him with their incantatory
metre. The swift made a semicircular turn

over the hills, then, like a feathery lure, she
bobbed over the wake, the same distance from the stern.
He felt she was guiding and not following them

ever since she'd leapt from the blossoms of the froth
hooked to his heart, as if her one, arrowing aim
was his happiness and that was blessing enough.

Steadily she kept her distance. He said the name
that he knew her by—*l'hirondelle des Antilles*,
the tag on Maud's quilt. The mate jigged the bamboo rods

from which the baits trawled. Then it frightened Achille
that this was no swallow but the bait of the gods,
that she had seen the god's body torn from its hill.

II

The horned island sank. This meant they were far out,
perhaps twenty miles, over the unmarked fathoms
where the midshipman watched the frigate come about,

where no anchor has enough rope and no plummet plumbs.
His cold heart was heaving in the ancestral swell
of the ocean that had widened around the last

point where the Trades bent the almonds like a candle-
flame. He stood as the swift suddenly shot past
the hull, so closely that he thought he heard a cry

from the small parted beak, and he saw the whole world
globed in the passing sorrow of her sleepless eye.
The mate never saw her. He watched as Achille furled

both oars into one oar and laid them parallel
in the grave of *In God We Troust*, like man and wife,
like grandmother and grandfather with ritual

solicitude, then stood balancing with a knife
as firm as a gommier rooted in its own ground.
"You okay?" he said, speaking to the swaying mast.

And these were the noble and lugubrious names
under the rocking shadow of *In God We Troust*:
Habal, swept in a gale overboard; Winston James,

commonly known as *"Toujours Sou"* or "Always Soused,"
whose body disappeared, some claimed in a vapour
of white rum or l'absinthe; Herald Chastenet, plaiter

of lobster-pots, whose alias was *"Fourmi Rouge,"*
i.e., "Red Ant," who was terrified of water
but launched a skiff one sunrise with white-rum courage

to conquer his fear. Some fishermen could not swim.
Dorcas Henry could not, but they learnt this later
searching the pronged rocks for whelks, where they found him,

for some reason clutching a starfish. There were others
whom Achille had heard of, mainly through Philoctete,
and, of course, the nameless bones of all his brothers

drowned in the crossing, plus a Midshipman Plunkett.
He stood like a mast amidships, remembering them,
in the lace wreaths of the Caribbean anthem.

Achille looked up at the sun, it was vertical
as an anchor-rope. Its ring ironed his hot skull
like a flat iron, singeing his cap with its smell.

No action but stasis. He is riding the swell
of the line now. He lets the angling oars idle
in their wooden oarlocks. He sprinkles the scorched sail

stitched from old flour sacks and tied round the middle
with seawater from the calabash to keep it supple,
scooping with one hand over the rocking gunwale

with the beat of habit, a hand soaked in its skill,
or the stitches could split the seams, and the ply
of its knots rot from this heat. Then, as Achille

sprinkles the flour sack, he watches it dry rapidly
in a sun like a hot iron flattening his skull,
and staggers with the calabash. The tied bundle

huddles like a corpse. *Oui, Bon Dieu!* I go hurl
it overside. Out of the depths of his ritual
baptism something was rising, some white memory

of a midshipman coming up close to the hull,
a white turning body, and this water go fill
with them, turning tied canvases, not sharks, but all

corpses wrapped like the sail, and ice-sweating Achille
in the stasis of his sunstroke looked as each swell
disgorged them, in tens, in hundreds, and his soul

sickened and was ill. His jaw slackened. A gull
screeched whirling backwards, and it was the tribal
sorrow that Philoctete could not drown in alcohol.

It was not forgetful as the sea-mist or the crash
of breakers on the crisp beaches of Senegal
or the Guinea coast. He reached for the calabash

and poured it streaming over his boiling skull,
then sat back and tried to settle the wash
of bilge in his stomach. Then he began to pull

at the knots in the sail. Meanwhile, that fool
his mate went on quietly setting the fishpot.
Time is the metre, memory the only plot.

His shoulders are knobs of ebony. The back muscles
can bulge like porpoises leaping out of this line
from the gorge of our memory. His hard fists enclose

its mossed rope as bearded as a love-vine
or a blind old man, tight as a shark's jaws,
wrenching the weight, then loosening it again

as the line saws his palms' sealed calluses,
the logwood thighs anchor against the fast drain
of the trough, and here is my tamer of horses,

our only inheritance that elemental noise
of the windward, unbroken breakers, Ithaca's
or Africa's, all joining the ocean's voice,

because this is the Atlantic now, this great design
of the triangular trade. Achille saw the ghost
of his father's face shoot up at the end of the line.

Achille stared in pious horror at the bound canvas
and could not look away, or loosen its burial knots.
Then, for the first time, he asked himself who he was.

He was lured by the swift the way trolling water
mesmerizes a fisherman who stares at the
fake metal fish as the lace troughs widen and close.

III

Outrunner of flying fish, under the geometry
of the hidden stars, her wire flashed and faded
taut as a catch, this mite of the sky-touching sea

towing a pirogue a thousand times her own weight
with a hummingbird's electric wings, this engine
that shot ahead of each question like an answer,

once Achille had questioned his name and its origin.
She touched both worlds with her rainbow, this frail dancer
leaping the breakers, this dart of the meridian.

She could loop the stars with a fishline, she tired
porpoises, she circled epochs with her outstretched span;
she gave a straight answer when one was required,

she skipped the dolphin's question, she stirred every spine
of a sea-egg tickling your palm rank with the sea;
she shut the ducts of a starfish, she was the mind-

messenger, and her speed outdarted Memory.
She was the swift that he had seen in the cedars
in the foam of clouds, when she had shot across

the blue ridges of the waves, to a god's orders,
and he, at the beck of her beak, watched the bird hum
the whipping Atlantic, and felt he was headed home.

Where whales burst into flower and sails turn back
from a tiring horizon, she shot with curled feet
close to her wet belly, round-eyed, her ruddering beak

towing *In God We Troust* so fast that he felt his feet
drumming on the ridged keel-board, its shearing motion
whirred by the swift's flywheel into open ocean.

CHAPTER XXV

I

Mangroves, their ankles in water, walked with the canoe.
The swift, racing its browner shadow, screeched, then veered
into a dark inlet. It was the last sound Achille knew

from the other world. He feathered the paddle, steered
away from the groping mangroves, whose muddy shelves
slipped warted crocodiles, slitting the pods of their eyes;

then the horned river-horses rolling over themselves
could capsize the keel. It was like the African movies
he had yelped at in childhood. The endless river unreeled

those images that flickered into real mirages:
naked mangroves walking beside him, knotted logs
wriggling into the water, the wet, yawning boulders

of oven-mouthed hippopotami. A skeletal warrior
stood up straight in the stern and guided his shoulders,
clamped his neck in cold iron, and altered the oar.

Achille wanted to scream, he wanted the brown water
to harden into a road, but the river widened ahead
and closed behind him. He heard screeching laughter

in a swaying tree, as monkeys swung from the rafter
of their tree-house, and the bared sound rotted the sky
like their teeth. For hours the river gave the same show

for nothing, the canoe's mouth muttered its lie.
The deepest terror was the mud. The mud with no shadow
like the clear sand. Then the river coiled into a bend.

He saw the first signs of men, tall sapling fishing-stakes;
he came into his own beginning and his end,
for the swiftness of a second is all that memory takes.

Now the strange, inimical river surrenders its stealth
to the sunlight. And a light inside him wakes,
skipping centuries, ocean and river, and Time itself.

And God said to Achille, "Look, I giving you permission
to come home. Is I send the sea-swift as a pilot,
the swift whose wings is the sign of my crucifixion.

And thou shalt have no God should in case you forgot
my commandments." And Achille felt the homesick shame
and pain of his Africa. His heart and his bare head

were bursting as he tried to remember the name
of the river- and the tree-god in which he steered,
whose hollow body carried him to the settlement ahead.

II

He remembered this sunburnt river with its spindly
stakes and the peaked huts platformed above the spindles
where thin, naked figures as he rowed past looked unkindly

or kindly in their silence. The silence an old fence kindles
in a boy's heart. They walked with his homecoming
canoe past bonfires in a scorched clearing near the edge

of the soft-lipped shallows whose noise hurt his drumming
heart as the pirogue slid its raw, painted wedge
towards the crazed sticks of a vine-fastened pier.

The river was sloughing its old skin like a snake
in wrinkling sunshine; the sun resumed its empire
over this branch of the Congo; the prow found its stake

in the river and nuzzled it the way that a piglet
finds its favourite dug in the sweet-grunting sow,
and now each cheek ran with its own clear rivulet

of tears, as Achille, weeping, fastened the bow
of the dugout, wiped his eyes with one dry palm,
and felt a hard hand help him up the shaking pier.

Half of me was with him. One half with the midshipman
by a Dutch canal. But now, neither was happier
or unhappier than the other. An old man put an arm

around Achille, and the crowd, chattering, followed both.
They touched his trousers, his undershirt, their hands
scrabbling the texture, as a kitten does with cloth,

till they stood before an open hut. The sun stands
with expectant silence. The river stops talking,
the way silence sometimes suddenly turns off a market.

The wind squatted low in the grass. A man kept walking
steadily towards him, and he knew by that walk it
was himself in his father, the white teeth, the widening hands.

III

He sought his own features in those of their life-giver,
and saw two worlds mirrored there: the hair was surf
curling round a sea-rock, the forehead a frowning river,

as they swirled in the estuary of a bewildered love,
and Time stood between them. The only interpreter
of their lips' joined babble, the river with the foam,

and the chuckles of water under the sticks of the pier,
where the tribe stood like sticks themselves, reversed
by reflection. Then they walked up to the settlement,

and it seemed, as they chattered, everything was rehearsed
for ages before this. He could predict the intent
of his father's gestures; he was moving with the dead.

Women paused at their work, then smiled at the warrior
returning from his battle with smoke, from the kingdom
where he had been captured, they cried and were happy.

Then the fishermen sat near a large tree under whose dome
stones sat in a circle. His father said:

"Afo-la-be,"

touching his own heart.

"In the place you have come from

what do they call you?"

Time translates.

Tapping his chest,

the son answers:

"Achille." The tribe rustles, "Achille."
Then, like cedars at sunrise, the mutterings settle.

AFOLABE
Achille. What does the name mean? I have forgotten the one
that I gave you. But it was, it seems, many years ago.
What does it mean?

ACHILLE
Well, I too have forgotten.

Everything was forgotten. You also. I do not know.
The deaf sea has changed around every name that you gave
us; trees, men, we yearn for a sound that is missing.

AFOLABE
A name means something. The qualities desired in a son,
and even a girl-child; so even the shadows who called
you expected one virtue, since every name is a blessing,

since I am remembering the hope I had for you as a child.
Unless the sound means nothing. Then you would be nothing.
Did they think you were nothing in that other kingdom?

ACHILLE

I do not know what the name means. It means something,
maybe. What's the difference? In the world I come from
we accept the sounds we were given. Men, trees, water.

AFOLABE

And therefore, Achille, if I pointed and I said, There
is the name of that man, that tree, and this father,
would every sound be a shadow that crossed your ear,

without the shape of a man or a tree? What would it be?
(And just as branches sway in the dusk from their fear
of amnesia, of oblivion, the tribe began to grieve.)

ACHILLE

What would it be? I can only tell you what I believe,
or had to believe. It was prediction, and memory,
to bear myself back, to be carried here by a swift,

or the shadow of a swift making its cross on water,
with the same sign I was blessed with, with the gift
of this sound whose meaning I still do not care to know.

AFOLABE

No man loses his shadow except it is in the night,
and even then his shadow is hidden, not lost. At the glow
of sunrise, he stands on his own name in that light.

When he walks down to the river with the other fishermen
his shadow stretches in the morning, and yawns, but you,
if you're content with not knowing what our names mean,

then I am not Afolabe, your father, and you look through
my body as the light looks through a leaf. I am not here
or a shadow. And you, nameless son, are only the ghost

of a name. Why did I never miss you until you returned?
Why haven't I missed you, my son, until you were lost?
Are you the smoke from a fire that never burned?

There was no answer to this, as in life. Achille nodded,
the tears glazing his eyes, where the past was reflected
as well as the future. The white foam lowered its head.

CHAPTER LXIV

I

I sang of quiet Achille, Afolabe's son,
who never ascended in an elevator,
who had no passport, since the horizon needs none,

never begged nor borrowed, was nobody's waiter,
whose end, when it comes, will be a death by water
(which is not for this book, which will remain unknown

and unread by him). I sang the only slaughter
that brought him delight, and that from necessity—
of fish, sang the channels of his back in the sun.

I sang our wide country, the Caribbean Sea.
Who hated shoes, whose soles were as cracked as a stone,
who was gentle with ropes, who had one suit alone,

whom no man dared insult and who insulted no one,
whose grin was a white breaker cresting, but whose frown
was a growing thunderhead, whose fist of iron

would do me a greater honour if it held on
to my casket's oarlocks than mine lifting his own
when both anchors are lowered in the one island,

but now the idyll dies, the goblet is broken,
and rainwater trickles down the brown cheek of a jar
from the clay of Choiseul. So much left unspoken

by my chirping nib! And my earth-door lies ajar.
I lie wrapped in a flour-sack sail. The clods thud
on my rope-lowered canoe. Rasping shovels scrape

a dry rain of dirt on its hold, but turn your head
when the sea-almond rattles or the rust-leaved grape
from the shells of my unpharaonic pyramid

towards paper shredded by the wind and scattered
like white gulls that separate their names from the foam
and nod to a fisherman with his khaki dog

that skitters from the wave-crash, then frown at his form
for one swift second. In its earth-trough, my pirogue
with its brass-handled oarlocks is sailing. Not from

but with them, with Hector, with Maud in the rhythm
of her beds trowelled over, with a swirling log
lifting its mossed head from the swell; let the deep hymn

of the Caribbean continue my epilogue;
may waves remove their shawls as my mourners walk home
to their rusted villages, good shoes in one hand,

passing a boy who walked through the ignorant foam,
and saw a sail going out or else coming in,
and watched asterisks of rain puckering the sand.

II

You can see Helen at the Halcyon. She is dressed
in the national costume: white, low-cut bodice,
with frilled lace at the collar, just a cleft of a breast

for the customers when she places their orders
on the shields of the tables. They can guess the rest
under the madras skirt with its golden borders

and the flirtatious knot of the madras head-tie.
She pauses between the tables, holding a tray
over her stomach to hide the wave-rounded sigh

of her pregnancy. There is something too remote
about her stillness. Women study her beauty,
but turn their faces away if their eyes should meet,

like an ebony carving. But if she should swerve
that silhouette hammered out of the sea's metal
like a profile on a shield, its sinuous neck

longing like a palm's, you might recall that battle
for which they named an island or the heaving wreck
of the *Ville de Paris* in her foam-frilled bodice,

or just think, "What a fine local woman!" and her
head will turn when you snap your fingers, the slow eyes
approaching you with the leisure of a panther

through white tables with palm-green iron umbrellas,
past children wading with water-wings in the pool;
and Africa strides, not alabaster Hellas,

and half the world lies open to show its black pearl.
She waits for your order and you lower your eyes
away from hers that have never carried the spoil

of Troy, that never betrayed horned Menelaus
or netted Agamemnon in their irises.
But the name Helen had gripped my wrist in its vise

to plunge it into the foaming page. For three years,
phantom hearer, I kept wandering to a voice
hoarse as winter's echo in the throat of a vase!

Like Philoctete's wound, this language carries its cure,
its radiant affliction; reluctantly now,
like Achille's, my craft slips the chain of its anchor,

moored to its cross as I leave it; its nodding prow
lettered as simply, ribbed in our native timber,
riding these last worried lines; its rhythm agrees

that all it forgot a swift made it remember
since that green sunrise of axes and laurel-trees,
till the sunset chars it, slowly, to an ember.

And Achille himself had been one of those children
whose voices are surf under a galvanized roof;
sheep bleating in the schoolyard; a Caribbean

whose woolly crests were the backs of the Cyclops's flock,
with the smart man under one's belly. Blue stories
we recited as children lifted with the rock

of Polyphemus. From a plaster Omeros
the smoke and the scarves of mares' tails, continually
chalked associate phantoms across our own sky.

III

Out of their element, the thrashing mackerel
thudded, silver, then leaden. The vermilion scales
of snappers faded like sunset. The wet, mossed coral

sea-fans that winnowed weeds in the wiry water
stiffened to bony lace, and the dripping tendrils
of an octopus wrung its hands at the slaughter

from the gutting knives. Achille unstitched the entrails
and hurled them on the sand for the palm-ribbed mongrels
and the sawing flies. As skittish as hyenas

the dogs trotted, then paused, angling their muzzles
sideways to gnaw on trembling legs, then lift a nose
at more scavengers. A triumphant Achille,

his hands gloved in blood, moved to the other canoes
whose hulls were thumping with fishes. In the spread seine
the silvery mackerel multiplied the noise

of coins in a basin. The copper scales, swaying,
were balanced by one iron tear; then there was peace.
They washed their short knives, they wrapped the flour-bag sails,

then they helped him haul *In God We Troust* back in place,
jamming logs under its keel. He felt his muscles
unknotting like rope. The nets were closing their eyes,

sagging on bamboo poles near the concrete depot.
In the standpipe's sandy trough aching Achille
washed sand from his heels, then tightened the brass spigot

to its last drop. An immense lilac emptiness
settled the sea. He sniffed his name in one armpit.
He scraped dry scales off his hands. He liked the odours

of the sea in him. Night was fanning its coalpot
from one catching star. The No Pain lit its doors
in the village. Achille put the wedge of dolphin

that he'd saved for Helen in Hector's rusty tin.
A full moon shone like a slice of raw onion.
When he left the beach the sea was still going on.

From

THE BOUNTY

(1997)

Miraculous as when a small cloud of cabbage-whites
circles a bush, the first flakes of the season
spun over Brookline, on Beacon; the afternoon lights
would come on by four, but everyone said, "So soon?"
at the multiplying butterflies, though it was late November,
but also because they had forgotten the miracle,
though the trees were stricken and brief day's ember
didn't catch in their firewood; they did not recall
the elation of flakes and butterflies that their element
is a joy quickly forgotten, and thus with the fall
certainly gone, the leaves dimmed, their flare spent,
the old metaphor whispered to everyone's mouth
about age, white hair, the Arctic virginity of death,
that the flakes spun like ashes; but before my heart fled south,
my farewell confirmed by the signature of your breath,
white butterflies circling, settling in your hair, that could soothe
your closed eyelids trembling like cabbage-whites
on my island road, the sea's scales stuttering in the sun.

14

Never get used to this; the feathery, swaying casuarinas,
the morning silent light on shafts of bright grass,
the growling *Aves* of the ocean, the white lances of the marinas,
the surf fingering its beads, hail heron and gull full of grace,
since that is all you need to do now at your age
and its coming serene extinction like the light on the shale
at sunset, and your gift fading out of this page;
your soul travelled the one horizon like a quiet snail,
infinity behind it, infinity ahead of it,
and all that it knew was this craft, all that it wanted—
what did it know of death? Only what you had read of it,
that it was like a flame blown out in a lowered lantern,
a night, but without these stars, the prickle of planets, lights
like a vast harbour, or devouring oblivion;
never get used to this, the great moon on these studded nights
that make the heart stagger; and the stirring lion
of the headland. This is why you have ended, to pass,
praising the feathery swaying of the casuarinas
and those shudderings of thanks that so often descended,
the evening light in the shafts of feathery grass,
the lances fading, then the lights of the marinas,
the yachts studying their reflections in black glass.

Alphaeus Prince. What a name! He was one of the Princes.
He died, a boy, as so many princes did in literature,
in English history, of a fierce obscure disease,
a regal and privileged fever, we envied him the Tower,
the ermine and mink and the orb; he so simply entered
legend, which death was to us children suffering
that radiated glory that withheld its own crown
until Alphaeus Prince one day would be Alphaeus King,
which was not ordained by fate, so that the promise and prize
of his name would always float over each bowed head
as we imagined his smooth brown skin, his large black eyes
closed in the superior knowledge of being dead.
Brighter than me, but darker (that mattered then
and still does, not here so much, but the world beyond).
What was his future in a world that was ruled by men
Milton and Cromwell's colour? Princes and angels were blond.
Fifty years later, why should the name spring
into mind, or aim like a shaft of light in the mind
further back than the friends I know who have been dying
as if from some medieval plague. This morning the sea-wind
is fresh, the island shines in light, and I think of a boy
I loved for his beauty, his wit, his eyes, which to me carried
a glint of their brevity, whose name still carries joy
in it, and who made death a gift that we quietly envied.

The sublime always begins with the chord "And then I saw,"
following which apocalyptic cumuli curl and divide
and the light with its silently widening voice might say:
"From that whirling rose that broadens its rings in the void
here come my horsemen: Famine, Plague, Death, and War."
Then the clouds are an avalanche of skulls torrentially rolling
over a still, leaden sea. And here beginneth the season
when the storm-birds panic differently and a bell starts tolling
in the mind from the rocking sea-wash (there is no such sound),
but that is the sway of things, which has the necks of the coconuts
bending like grazing giraffes. I stood on the dark sand
and then I saw that darkness which I gradually accepted
grow startling in its joy, its promised anonymity
in its galloping breakers, in time and the space that kept it
immortal and changing without the least thought of me,
the serrated turret of a rock and the white horse that leapt it,
that spumed and vaulted with the elation of its horsemen,
a swallowing of a turmoil of a vertiginous chaos,
the delight of a leaf in a sudden gust of force when
between grey channels the islands are slowly erased
and one dare not ask of the thunder what is its cause.
Let it be written: The dark days also I have praised.

Praise to the rain, eraser of picnics, praise the grey cloud
that makes every headland a ghost, and the guttering belch-
braided water, praise to the rain and her slow shroud,
she is the muse of Amnesia which is another island,
spectral and adrift where those we still love exist
but in another sense, that this shore cannot understand,
for reminding us that all substance thins into mist
and has its vague frontiers, the country of memory
and, as in Rimbaud, the idea of eternity,
is a razed horizon when the sky and the sea are mixed
and the solid disappears like the dead into essences
which is the loud message of the martial advancing rain
with its lances and mass and—sometimes alarming our senses—
the kettledrums of advancing thunder. Before her the grain
bows and darkens, the tide cowers then rises, the air
becomes palpable, and our nerves assemble for a siege
in the shut eyes and clamped doors of our body, her hair
horizontal in the wind blown back like the surge,
the casuarinas whine and sway in the wind, two drops
startle the flesh and the sun withdraws behind drapes
like a king or a president on the palace balcony
who hears the roar of a square and thinks it is only
the rain, it will pass, tomorrow will be sunny,
praise to the rain its hoarse voice dissolver of shapes,
of the peaks of power, princes, and mountain slopes.

31 ITALIAN ECLOGUES

[*for Joseph Brodsky*]

I

On the bright road to Rome, beyond Mantua,
there were reeds of rice, and I heard, in the wind's elation,
the brown dogs of Latin panting alongside the car,
their shadows sliding on the verge in smooth translation,
past fields fenced by poplars, stone farms in character,
nouns from a schoolboy's text, Virgilian, Horatian,
phrases from Ovid passing in a green blur,
heading towards perspectives of noseless busts,
open-mouthed ruins, and roofless corridors
of Caesars whose second mantle is now the dust's,
and this voice that rustles out of the reeds is yours.
To every line there is a time and a season.
You refreshed forms and stanzas; these cropped fields are
your stubble grating my cheeks with departure,
grey irises, your corn-wisps of hair blowing away.
Say you haven't vanished, you're still in Italy.
Yeah. Very still. God. Still as the turning fields
of Lombardy, still as the white wastes of that prison
like pages erased by a regime. Though his landscape heals
the exile you shared with Naso, poetry is still treason
because it is truth. Your poplars spin in the sun.

At the end of this line there is an opening door
that gives on a blue balcony where a gull will settle
with hooked fingers, then, like an image leaving an idea,
beat in slow scansion across the hammered metal
of the afternoon sea, a sheet that my right hand steers—
a small sail making for Martinique or Sicily.
In the lilac-flecked distance, the same headlands rust
with flecks of houses blown from the spume of the trough,
and the echo of a gull where a gull's shadow raced
between sunlit seas. No cry is exultant enough
for my thanks, for my heart that flings open its hinges
and slants my ribs with light. At the end, a shadow
slower than a gull's over water lengthens, by inches,
and covers the lawn. There is the same high ardour
of rhetorical sunsets in Sicily as over Martinique,
and the same horizon underlines their bright absence,
the long-loved shining there who, perhaps, do not speak
from unutterable delight, since speech is for mortals,
since at the end of each sentence there is a grave
or the sky's blue door or, once, the widening portals
of our disenfranchised sublime. The one light we have
still shines on a spire or a conch-shell as it falls
and folds this page over with a whitening wave.

From

TIEPOLO'S HOUND

(2000)

(I)

1

They stroll on Sundays down Dronningens Street,
passing the bank and the small island shops

quiet as drawings, keeping from the heat
through Danish arches until the street stops

at the blue, gusting harbour, where like commas
in a shop ledger gulls tick the lined waves.

Sea-light on the cod barrels writes: *St. Thomas*,
the salt breeze brings the sound of Mission slaves

chanting deliverance from all their sins
in tidal couplets of lament and answer,

the horizon underlines their origins—
Pissarros from the ghetto of Braganza

who fled the white hoods of the Inquisition
for the bay's whitecaps, for the folding cross

of a white herring gull over the Mission
droning its passages from Exodus.

Before the family warehouse, near the Customs,
his uncle jerks the locks, rattling their chains,

and lifts his beard to where morning comes
across wide water to the Gentile mountains.

Out of the cobalt bay, her blunt bow cleaving
the rising swell that racing bitterns skip,

the mail boat moans. They feel their bodies leaving
the gliding island, not the blowing ship.

A mongrel follows them, black as its shadow,
nosing their shadows, scuttling when the bells

exult with pardon. Young Camille Pissarro
studies the schooners in their stagnant smells.

He and his starched Sephardic family,
followed from a nervous distance by the hound,

retrace their stroll through Charlotte Amalie
in silence as its Christian bells resound,

sprinkling the cobbles of Dronningens Gade,
the shops whose jalousies in blessing close,

through repetitions of the oval shade
of Danish arches to their high wooden house.

The Synagogue of Blessing and Peace and Loving Deeds
is shut for this Sabbath. The mongrel cowers

through a park's railing. The bells recede.
The afternoon is marked by cedar flowers.

Their street of letters fades, this page of print
in the bleached light of last century recalls

with the sharp memory of a mezzotint:
days of cane carts, the palms' high parasols.

2

My wooden window frames the Sunday street
which a black dog crosses into Woodford Square.

From a stone church, tribal voices repeat
the tidal couplets of lament and prayer.

Behind the rusted lances of a railing
stands the green ribbed fan of a Traveller's Tree;

an iron gate, its croton hedge availing
itself of every hue, screeches on entry.

Walk down the path, enter the yawning stone,
its walls as bare as any synagogue

of painted images. The black congregation
frown in the sun at the sepulchral dog.

There was a *shul* in old-time Port of Spain,
but where its site precisely was is lost

in the sunlit net of maps whose lanes contain
a spectral faith, white as the mongrel's ghost.

Stiller the palms on Sunday, fiercer the grass,
blacker the shade under the boiling trees,

sharper the shadows, quieter the grace
of afternoon, the city's emptiness.

And over the low hills there is the haze
of heat and a smell of rain in the noise

of trees lightly thrashing where one drop has
singed the scorched asphalt as more petals rise.

A silent city, blest with emptiness
like an engraving. Ornate fretwork eaves,

and the heat rising from the pitch in wires,
from empty back yards with calm breadfruit leaves,

their walls plastered with silence, the same streets
with the same sharp shadows, laced verandahs closed

in torpor, until afternoon repeats
the long light with its croton-coloured crowds

in the Savannah, not the Tuileries, but
still the Rock Gardens' brush-point cypresses

like a Pissarro canvas, past the shut
gate of the President's Palace, flecked dresses

with gull cries, white flowers and cricketers,
coconut carts, a frilled child with the hoop

of the last century, and, just as it was
in Charlotte Amalie, a slowly creaking sloop.

Laventille's speckled roofs, just as it was
in Cazabon's day, the great Savannah cedars,

the silent lanes at sunrise, parked cars
quiet at their culverts, trainers, owners, breeders

before they moved the paddocks, the low roofs
under the low hills, the sun-sleeved Savannah

under the elegance of grass-muffled hooves,
the cantering snort, the necks reined in; a

joy that was all smell, fresh dung; the jokes
of the Indian grooms, that civilizing

culture of horses, the *fin de siècle* spokes
of trotting carriages, and egrets rising,

as across olive hills a flock of pigeons,
keeping its wide ellipse over dark trees

to the Five Islands, soundlessly joins
its white flecks to the sails on quiet seas.

The white line of chalk birds draws on an Asia
of white-lime walls, prayer flags, and minarets,

blackbirds bring Guinea to thorns of acacia,
and in the saffron of Tiepolo sunsets,

the turbulent paradise of bright rotundas
over aisles of cane, and censer-carried mists,

then, blazing from the ridges of Maracas—
the croton hues of the Impressionists.

3

On my first trip to the Modern I turned a corner,
rooted before the ridged linen of a Cézanne.

A still life. I thought how clean his brushes were!
Across that distance light was my first lesson.

I remember stairs in couplets. The Metropolitan's
marble authority, I remember being

stunned as I studied the exact expanse
of a Renaissance feast, the art of seeing.

Then I caught a slash of pink on the inner thigh
of a white hound entering the cave of a table,

so exact in its lucency at *The Feast of Levi*,
I felt my heart halt. Nothing, not the babble

of the unheard roar that rose from the rich
pearl-lights embroidered on ballooning sleeves,

sharp beards, and gaping goblets, matched the bitch
nosing a forest of hose. So a miracle leaves

its frame, and one epiphanic detail
illuminates an entire epoch:

a medal by Holbein, a Vermeer earring, every scale
of a walking mackerel by Bosch, their sacred shock.

Between me and Venice the thigh of a hound;
my awe of the ordinary, because even as I write,

paused on a step of this couplet, I have never found
its image again, a hound in astounding light.

Everything blurs. Even its painter. Veronese
or Tiepolo in a turmoil of gesturing flesh,

drapery, columns, arches, a crowded terrace,
a balustrade with leaning figures. In the mesh

of Venetian light on its pillared arches
Paolo Veronese's *Feast in the House of Levi*

opens on a soundless page, but no shaft catches
my memory: one stroke for a dog's thigh!

4

But isn't that the exact perspective of loss,
that the loved one's features blur, in dimming detail,

the smile with its dimpled corners, her teasing voice
rasping with affection, as Time draws its veil,

until all you remember are her young knees
gleaming from an olive dress, her way of walking,

as if on a page of self-arranging trees,
hair a gold knot, rose petals silently talking?

I catch an emerald sleeve, light knits her hair,
in a garland of sculpted braids, her burnt cheeks;

catch her sweet breath, be the blest one near her
at that Lucullan table, lean when she speaks,

as clouds of centuries pass over the brilliant ground
of the fresco's meats and linen, while her wrist

in my forced memory caresses an arched hound,
as all its figures melt in the fresco's mist.

(VII)

1

Falling from chimneys, an exhausted arrow—
he watched a swallow settling on its ledge;

its wings wrote "Paris" from the name "Pissarro,"
a brush lettering a cloud's canvas edge.

The studio was cavernously cold. In their
jars, bristles froze, but he was determined,

when spectres snubbed him in the ashen air,
to erase his island as the knifing wind

sharpened its blade on lampposts, that homecoming
glowed from the orange windows of his street,

groping up steps to feel his body humming
like the stove's belly with malarial heat.

Needles of icy rain, swivelling slush,
head down against their onslaught were still his

more than the snowdrops on an evergreen bush,
those lamps in daylight, the stiff smoke of chimneys.

Wasn't the old persecution still possession?
His history emerged in the half-light

of Rembrandt's gaze, and Saskia's thighs that shone,
brightening a pool, his heritage by right.

Silk hats, their asphalt sheen, hazed Notre Dame,
wet, wriggling reflections, chestnuts in braziers,

horse dung and drizzle, all were his to claim
by drawing on the fog's careful erasures.

A brushstroke flicks a whip, and a carriage lurches
from the leaf-shade of lindens, a grey stallion

clops down lime avenues, past famous churches
joining hyphens in a sprinkling carillon,

a page of the boulevard opens, smoke, cirrus above
Baudelaire's *"fourmillante cité,"* a bursting anthill

of crowds and carriages, quick strokes make them move,
in time with bell and whip, stanza and canticle.

The lark of an acolyte's voice climbs from the choir
from a city that worships Sundays, parks, and prams,

and the clouds of a Tiepolo ceiling, their saffron fire,
a sky that it shares with his island's rusted palms.

2

O, the exclamation of white roses, of a wet
grey day of glazed pavements, the towers

in haze of Notre Dame's silhouette
in the Easter drizzle, lines banked with flowers

and umbrellas flowering, then bobbing like mushrooms
in the soup-steaming fog! Paris looked edible:

salads of parks, a bouillabaisse of fumes
from its steaming trees in the incredible

fragrance of April; and all this would pass
into mist, even cherishable mud, the delicate

entrance of tentative leaves and the grass
renewed when the sun opened its gate.

The Renaissance, brightening, had painted altars,
ceilings, cupolas, feasts with an arched dog,

this city's painters, the guild in her ateliers
made her sublime and secular as fog.

3

Since light was simply particles in air,
and shadow shared the spectrum, strokes of paint

are phrases that haphazardly cohere
around a point to build an argument,

vision was not the concentrated gaze
that took in every detail at a glance.

Time, petrified in every classic canvas,
denied the frailty of the painter's hands,

acquired an intimacy with its origin, Claude,
David, and the Venetian schools presumed

a privilege given by the gods or God,
while Time's blasphemous fire consumed, consumed.

Now sunlight is splintered and even shade is entered
as part of the prism, and except for its defiant

use in Manet, black is a coiled tube drying
from neglect, the classical drama of painting is interred

with Courbet's *The Funeral*. Landscape as theatre,
shadow as melodrama without damnation,

buried with the painter's belief in a Creator
who balanced evil and light in one dimension,

shade lost its moral contrast, doubt disappears
in the moment's exaltations, in flowers and loaves

as a loaf in Chardin belittles the girls in Greuze
with its solid denial, the death behind his still lifes.

In those still lifes, where dying rings like crystal
from glasses polished by a servant's breath,

lay the sweet pain of the Impressionists. All
natures-morts are altars laid for Death.

The metallic shine of a gaping mackerel,
the ring in its dead eye like a Vermeer earring;

that highlight on its skin sharpening smell.
There mastery lay in Manet, the same daring

that caught the vermilion light in a hound's thigh,
one stroke on the dog and the staring mackerel,

the spectral animal at *The Feast of Levi*,
licking her outstretched hand, shared the one skill.

But what conviction was carried in a sketch,
and patchy impasto surfaces with dim drawing?

What authority granted the privilege
of blurring, dissolving, ignoring form, outlawing

detail of trees without Corot's feathery grace?
Physics had analysed light into particles floating

and the Pointillist muse was Science; all space
was a concentration of dots, picnickers boating

on the summer Seine, dogs, parasols. Their refusers
rejected this change of vision, of deities; theories

instead of faith, geometry, not God. Their accusers
saw them as shallow heretics, unorthodox painters

using wriggles for tree trunks, charred twigs for figures,
crooked horizons, shadows streaked with purple;

they were the Academy's outcasts, its niggers
from barbarous colonies, a contentious people!

They followed impulse, with no concern for their craft,
geese that lacked the concentration of swans,

their brushstrokes wriggling necks. The Salon laughed
as it locked them out. Sketches. Impressions.

They were heretical in their delight,
there was no deity outdoors, no altar,

in the rose window of the iris, light
was their faith, a shaft in an atelier.

(XXII)

1

One dawn I woke up to the gradual terror
that all I had written of the hound was false.

I had pursued a melody of error,
my craft seduced by the twin siren calls

of Memory changing to Imagination,
of Reason into Rhyme. I knew I stood

before the uproar of a feast. Its station
was Venice, unvisited. Its poles were my dark wood,

from which the hound, now a chained Cerberus, growled
and lunged its treble heads at Accuracy,

a simple fact made myth, and the myth fouled
by its demonic piss. Tiepolo, Veronese,

the image I had cherished made no sense,
my memory's transference of their frescoes

meant that I never learnt the difference
between Veronese's gift and Tiepolo's.

And yet I hold my ground and hold it till
I trace the evasive hound beyond my fear

that it never existed, that exhaustion will
claim action as illusion, from despair.

Because if both Venetians painted frescoes,
then what I thought I saw had to be panels

or canvas seamed, but still the image grows
with more conviction there and nowhere else.

Then how could I be standing in two places,
first, in a Venice I had never seen,

despite its sharpness of prong-bearded faces,
then at the Metropolitan? What did the dog mean?

2

Over the years I abandoned the claim
of a passion which, if it existed, naturally faded

from my island Pissarro, rooted in his fame,
a smoke wisp on the Seine, his exile dictated

by a fiction that sought from him discipleship
in light and affection for our shacks and ridges

touched by crepuscular orange. No black steamship
roiled in its wake a pain that was ever his;

no loss of St. Thomas. Our characters are blent
not by talent but by climate and calling. Cézanne's

signing his work, *Pupil of Pissarro*, all I meant
was only affection's homage, and affection's

envy, benign as dusk arching over Charlotte Amalie,
and night, when centuries vanish, or when dawns rise

on the golden alleys of Paris, Castries, or Italy,
ceilings of Tiepolo or Veronese in changing skies.

A change of Muses, a change of light and customs,
of crooked tracks for avenues of bricks for straw,

change fiddling orchestras for firelit drums,
they were never his people, we were there to draw.

They, and everything else. Our native grace
is still a backward bending, out of fashion

in theatres and galleries; an island race
damned to the provincialities of passion.

My Muses pass, in their earth-rooted stride,
basket-balancing illiterate women, their load

an earthen vessel, its springs of joy inside,
pliant shadows striding down a mountain road.

In evening light a frangipani's antlers
darken over spume crests and become invisible

even to the full moon, and as dusk always does
for my eyes, and his lights bud on the black hill

to a cobbled brook's tireless recitation
in voluble pebbles as lucent as the ones

under the soles of the Baptist. Morning sun
on the corrugating stream over clean stones.

3

I thoroughly understand all he endures:
that sense of charity to a gifted stranger,

open to their gatherings, these voluble bores,
these brilliant jeerers. Friends are a danger,

proud of the tribal subtleties of their
suffering, its knot of meaning, of blood on the street

for an idea, their pain is privilege, a clear
tradition, proud in triumph, prouder in defeat,

for which they have made a language they share
in intellectual, odourless sweat.

Because they measure evil by the seasons, the clear
death of October, its massacre of leaves,

my monodic climate has no history. I hear
their bright applause for one another's lives.

My fault was ignorance of their History
and my contempt for it, they are my Old Masters,

sunlight and pastures, a tireless sea
with its one tense, one crest where the last was.

No scansion for the seasons, no epochs
for the fast scumbling surf, no dates

or decades for the salt-streaming rocks,
no spires or towers for the sailing frigates.

4

One sunrise I felt an ordinary
width of enlightenment in my motel,

at the Ramada Inn in Albany.
I was bent, writing, he was bent as well,

but in nineteenth-century St. Thomas
my body filled his pencilled silhouette

in arched Dronningens Gade, my trousers
rolled to the calves, in a sisal hat at the market

which I now tip in my acknowledgement
to him and Mr. Melbye. I'll be born

a hundred years later, but we're both bent
over this paper; I am being drawn,

anonymous as my own ancestor,
my Africa erased, if not his France,

the cobbled sunlit street with a dirt floor
and a quick sketch my one inheritance.

Then one noon where acacias shade the beach
I saw the parody of Tiepolo's hound

in the short salt grass, requiring no research,
but something still unpainted, on its own ground.

I had seen wolfhounds straining on the leash,
their haunches taut on tapestries of Spring;

now I had found, whose azure was a beach,
this tottering, abandoned, houseless thing.

A starved pup trembling by the hard sea,
far from the back yards of a village street.

She cried out in compassion. This was not the
cosseted lapdog in its satin seat,

not even Goya's mutt peering from a fissure
of that infernal chasm in the Prado,

but one that shook with local terror, unsure
of everything, even its shadow.

Its swollen belly was shivering from the heat
of starvation; she moaned and picked it up,

this was the mongrel's heir, not in a great
fresco, but bastardy, abandonment, and hope

and love enough perhaps to help it live
like all its breed, and charity, and care,

we set it down in the village to survive
like all my ancestry. The hound was here.

3

I looked beyond the tarmac. A bright field.
Late horizontal afternoon. Light, south

of the island. My grief unhealed
by the sacral egrets at a river's mouth

or the great geese crossing through my face
in the car window. I could see the foam

of Maria Island chafing at its base
and shadow-widowed sand. Four months from home.

I saw this promontory fringed with grass,
tall, bleached-white grass, the pennons of the drought

more straw than shoots. Then I knew where it was:
the blithely running sea around Vieux Fort,

the low cliffs that abruptly end in cactus,
in the agave's viridian detonations,

when we first painted and our shadows tracked us
up stone-loose paths towards the Atlantic's patience.

In the cold morning reeds disconsolate geese,
their great wings hammering the marsh-light silver,

launched their far squadrons in convulsive V's
south, south like arrows from the rushes' quiver!

Meadows and spires resumed from sinuous trains
in widening sunlight, while catarrhal geese

kept honking south, leaving brown mountains
jagged with ice, hard lakes, and iron trees.

Brown Italy, and azure Adriatic
of *faux-châteaux*, the mountains speckled ochre,

the snowline, and the shelving forests thick
as libraries, homesick for my acre,

for the green crests of Charlotte Amalie,
the yellow synagogue so far from Braganza,

for a mongrel in the shadows of an alley
on an island Sunday, a park's sunlit stanza.

4

Fall; and a cool blonde crosses Christopher—
braid coronet, skin colour: Veronese.

I stare. A brace of white hounds bolt from her
unleashed, to foam around Actaeon's knees.

In golden light, that *noli tangere*
which keeps its frame and distance on a street,

that utterance which has no words to say
as if it were a fresco will repeat

an old division. There's such a busy busy
biography between her and her clothes

(though less than those brocades of Veronese);
I have added more wolfhounds than Tiepolo's.

Hunched in its outline, the beast turned snarling
with one look from the wall, in recognition.

Then, flagging a leaf-yellow cab, my darling
yanked its neck with her hand, then they were gone.

From my tired taxi, rattling towards Kennedy,
the last defiant maples were on fire;

along a verge skeletal trees stood ready
for the thin winter sun, their usual fare.

The maple pyres, not merely fallen but curled
in their decrepitude, were bearing me

from autumn's acclamation of a world
flashing with its deciduous poetry,

and that blurred tapestry of incoherence
that passed for painting, from the age itself.

So many leaves blown from that stricken fence
of friends that have become spines on a shelf!

And then I turned and saw, racing the taxi,
through crossed twigs, billboards, a shrouding underpass,

with stalled, jerking traffic, the shadowy ecstasy
of a black mongrel loping behind glass.

1

The swallows flit in immortality,
moving yet motionless on the canvas roofs,

like signatures, memorials to his city,
swifter than strokes along a ledger's proofs

as when the V's of gulls skimmed the capped harbour,
lifting their cries above Dronningens Street,

and creaking canvas sails furled in their labour
of journeys finished in the Sunday heat.

Dusk in the islands. Gusts of swallows wheeling
over Paris and the furrows of Pontoise,

in couplets under a Tiepolo ceiling.
He enters the window frame. His gaze is yours.

Primed canvas, steaming mirror, this white page
where a drawing emerges. His portrait sighs

from a white fog. Pissarro in old age,
as we stand doubled in each other's eyes.

To endure affliction with no affection gone
seems to have been the settlement in those eyes,

whose lenses catch a glinting winter sun
on mansards and the rigid smoke of chimneys.

It is one of the mildest winters on record.
His glasses flash across the spray-burst beard,

a true timidity of disregard
from the halo of the bohemian beret.

Perhaps he wears it indoors from the cold,
the eyes are sunken, but their stare no sadder

under the arched brows than when the family strolled
the Danish stonework of Dronningens Gade;

the sceptic turned to a Sephardic sage,
rabbinical in his fragility,

since the snow's rapid strokes whitened a page
of canvas and we lost him to a city.

If the surf of apple orchards could be heard,
its murmur would come through this foaming page

where he chats with Cézanne in a flecked beard,
hat, boots, and staff; his palmer's pilgrimage.

Meanwhile, the palms, in their eternal summers,
rustling like children's lessons in the heat,

bring the occasional pilgrim to St. Thomas
to find the synagogue on its small street.

The soul is indivisible as air.
Supposedly, all things become a dream,

but we, as moving trees, must root somewhere,
and there our separation shows its seam,

in our attachment to the nurturing place
of earth, a buried string, a chattering stream

or still lagoon that holds our fading face,
that wrinkles from the egret's rising scream.

2

Time takes one hand and helps us up the stair,
Time draws the shades down on our clouding eyes;

they go together, painting and white hair,
a sea rock streaming, or skeined cirrus skies,

a mottled scalp of sun-receding snow
in piebald patches on a furrowed path,

in landscapes with no tenses, views that know
that now, as always, light is all we have.

Three years into the century, his sight
has failed, he paints from an open window

overlooking the street. One starry night
the vigil candles end. Dawn is his widow.

His brushes rest. Canvas and tombstone whiten.
Mattock and chisel hyphenate his fame.

The lindens flutter. The parentheses tighten
(and enclose Paris in Pissarro's name).

Help me to crease the pleats of an emerald sleeve
Giambattista Tiepolo, Paolo Veronese,

an idling wrist, the light through a cloud's sieve,
Camille Pissarro, on our beaches the breezy

light over our bays, help me to begin
when I set out again, at sixty-nine,

for the sacred villages. Dole out, in each tin,
clear linseed and redemptive turpentine.

I shall finish in a place whose only power
is the exploding spray along its coast,

its rotting asphalt and cantankerous poor
numb beyond resignation and its cost,

and I endure the gorgonizing glare
and toothless bitterness of destitution,

and hard soles scraping on a half-baked square,
though in his own day he saw no solution

except escape, as sprats race undersea
from a dividing shadow. What was his sin?

Where there's no trust there is no treachery.
The nets sag from black poles against the sun.

This is my peace, my salt, exulting acre:
there is no more Exodus, this is my Zion,

whose couplets race the furrowing wind, their maker,
with those homecoming sails on the horizon.

3

A dog barks in an unchanged neighbourhood,
Petit Valley marks the pilgrimage I have made,

its clouds spread in a linen gratitude
of fruit in a bowl, a pomme-arac's lilac shade,

and what lights the mind around sunlit corners
of Chumamonka Avenue's scorching asphalt

is a remembered happiness, now one as
grateful for the pardon of a deep fault;

passing thorns of forgiving bougainvillea,
raw scars on the old hill as age enjoys

the frames of a lost life again familiar—
Morne Coco, or the poplars of Pontoise.

For shaded corners of the Santa Cruz road
where sometimes you see horses through the trunks,

their hides reddish brown, umber, tan, coloured
like the trunks. For leaves and horses, thanks.

4

Let this page catch the last light on Becune Point,
lengthen the arched shadows of Charlotte Amalie,

to a prayer's curling smoke, and brass anoint
the branched menorah of a frangipani,

as the lights in the shacks bud orange across the Morne,
and are pillared in the black harbour. Stars fly close

as sparks, and the houses catch with bulb and lampion
to the Virgin, Veronese's and Tiepolo's.

Soon, against the smoky hillsides of Santa Cruz,
dusk will ignite the wicks of the immortelle,

parrots will clatter from the trees with raucous news
of the coming night, and the first star will settle.

Then all the sorrows that lay heavily on us,
the repeated failures, the botched trepidations

will pass like the lights on bridges at village corners
where shadows crouch under pierced constellations

whose name they have never learnt, as a sickle glow
rises over bamboos that repeat the round

of the charted stars, the Archer, aiming his bow,
the Bear, and the studded collar of Tiepolo's hound.

From

THE PRODIGAL

(2 0 0 4)

2

I

Chasms and fissures of the vertiginous Alps
through the plane window, meadows of snow
on powdery precipices, the cantons of cumuli
grumbling or closing, gasping falls of light
a steady and serene white-knuckled horror
of speckled white serrations, inconceivable
in repetition, spumy avalanches
of forgetting cloud, in the wrong heaven—
a paradise of ice and camouflage
of speeding seraphs' shadows down its slopes
under the metal, featherless wings, the noise
a violation of that pre-primal silence
white and without thought, my fear was white
and my belief obliterated—a black stroke
on a primed canvas, everything was white,
white was the colour of nothing, not the night,
my faith was strapped in. It could go no higher.
I doubted that there would be a blest descent
braking like threshing seraph's wings, to spire
and sun-shot field, wide, innocent.

The worst fear widened, to ask of the infinite:
How many more cathedral-spires? How many more
peaks of these ice-seized mountains, and towns
locked in by avalanches with their yellow lights
inside on their brilliant goods, with the clappers
of bells frozen by silence? How many small crows
like commas punctuating the drifts?
Infinite and repetitive as the ridges
patterned like okapi or jaguar, their white forests
are an opposite absolute world, a different life,
but more like a different death. The wanderer's cry
forms an O of terror but muted by the slanted snow

and a fear that is farther than panic. This,
whatever its lesson, is the tacit chorus
of the screaming mountains, the feathering alp,
the frozen ocean of oceanic roofs
above which hangs the white ogling horn—
skeletal tusk of a mastodon above white inns.

V

On the powdery ridges of the slopes were sheds
where cattle were byred in the winter darkness.
I imagined them blindly gurgitating their fodder,
and beyond them the vertiginous fissures
in the iron cold. There were the absolute,
these peaks, the pitch of temperature and terror,
polar rigidities that magnetized a child
these rocks bearded with icicles, crevasses
from Andersen's "Ice Maiden," Whittier's "Snow-Bound,"
this empire, this infernity of ice.
One afternoon, an eternity ago
in his warm island childhood in a jalousied room
with all the fire of daylight outside
in the bustling, black, barefoot street, his heart
was iced with terror, a frozen pond, in which
glazed faces started behind the glacial prose
of Hans Christian Andersen's "The Ice Maiden"
with its snow-locked horror, and that
afternoon has never left me. I did not know then that
she worked as a blond waitress in Zermatt.

I liked the precocious lamps in the evening.
I had never seen so much snow. It whitened night.
Out of this snow, like weeds that have survived,
came an assiduous fiction, one that the inns,
the gables shelved with white, the muted trails,
and (unavoidable) the sharp horn of the peak,
demanded of the ritual silence, a flare of light,

the flush of a warmed face, some elegy,
some cold enchantress, an ember's memory
of fire, provided since my young manhood
or earlier, of the Ice Maiden. She and the horn
were from the same white magic and when she came,
she lifted her head and the horn hooked my heart,
and the world magnified a greeting into love.

Wide meadows shot with a lemon light under the peaks,
the mineral glint of distant towns, the line of the plain
ending in the exclamation of a belfry!
Entering Lausanne, after the white ridges,
ochre scarps for a long while along the grey lake,
a lake so wide you could not see the other shore,
nor if souls walked along it, arms outstretched.
So many of them now on the other bank!

Then the old gentlemen at lunch in Lausanne
with suits of flawless cut, impeccable manners,
update of Rembrandt's *Syndics of the Drapers' Guild.*
I translated the pink, shaven faces of the Guild
to their dark-panelled and polished ancestry
of John the Baptist heads each borne on a saucer
of white lace, the loaded eyes, the thinning hair
over the white streaks of the foreheads, a syndicate
in which, far back, a negligible ancestor
might have been a member, greeting me
a product of his empire's miscegenation
in old St. Martin. I could find no trace.
Built in huge gilt frames I sometimes found myself
loitering among the markets and canals;
but in Geneva though I felt hung and mounted
in sepia rooms with a glazed stare.
Immense and grey, with its invisible shore.
The weather sounded like its name: Lausanne.
Thought furred and felt like an alderman's collar,
a chocolate stick for the voracious fog.

Irradiating outwards from that grey lake,
that grey which is the hue of historical peace
Geneva was the colour of a statesman's hair,
silvery and elegant and with a statesman's conscience,
banks and furled flags above the banks, and shoes
mirrored and quiet in deep-piled carpets.
The velvet, soft transactions of the world.
Stipple of farmhouse and fields, foothills dissolving
to lilac, violet shadows in the ridged furrows,
a spire slowly spinning away into Italy.

IV

I wanted to be able to write: "There is nothing like it,
to walk down the Via Veneto before sunrise."
And now, you think: he is going to describe it.
I am going to describe the benediction of June,
the grey cool spring air, its edges at *prima luce*,
too early for coffee from the hotel
and from the locked grids of last night's cafés,
the dew as wet as Pescara's the year before,
and the canvas umbrellas folded in their scabbards,
the reason being the difference in travel-time,
the difference being the night clerk yawning at the end
of his vigil, and the surly, early waiter,
then the long, unechoing empty street
that isn't as quiet as he had imagined,
with traffic building, the spiky palms
outside the American Embassy and two policemen
because of the threat of terrorists, the huge trees
against the pale buildings, the banks and arches
with their dirty flags; the lights still on
on certain buildings as the widening light
palely washed their façades, but the stillness
exactly like Gros Islet's, the sea and the village,
if not the vermilion buses under the trees
their lights still on, there, here it comes, the light
out of pearl, out of Piero della Francesca,
(you could tell he would mention a painter),
then slowly the whole fresco with the spring's gold
on Ministerio del Lavoro e delle Politiche Sociali
at whose gate a man came out and examined me
as I copied the name down, a bald young man
in an orange windbreaker who scowled
because of my colour and the terrorists,
and because my village was unimportantly beautiful

unlike his city and the Via Veneto,
its curved façades gamboge and ochre, grey stone,
the unnamed trees forming a gentle tunnel
over the buses, their lamps now out, vermilion, orange,
and what was missing was the smell of the sea
in the early morning on the small embankment,
but the palms as still in the dawn's docile tissue
Bus No. 63 L 90 Pugliese
whereas no echo in the name Gros Islet,
no literature, no history, at least until now.
Bus 116, lights on. On the Via Veneto.
Glides, like a fish, softly, or a turning leaf.

I lived in two villages: Greenwich and Gros Islet,
and loved both almost equally. One had the sea,
grey morning light along the waking water,
the other a great river, and if they asked
what country I was from I'd say, "The light
of that tree-lined sunrise down the Via Veneto."

6

III

"So, how was Italy?" My neighbor grinned.
Trim-bearded, elegant. He was Italian.
"Good. As usual. We were in Amalfi.
Next to a picturesque port called Vertigo."
He didn't get it. "Why didn't you stay longer?"
I said: "I have an island." "And it was calling you."
To say yes was stupidness, but it was true.
From the apartment I could see the Hudson.
Wide with its silent traffic, the silent buildings.

IV

Blue-grey morning, sunlight shaping Jersey,
and, magisterial, a white city gliding between buildings,
leaving the river for the Caribbean
its cargo: my longing. A high, immaculate ship.

I

I lay on the bed near the balcony in Guadalajara
and watched the afternoon wind stiffen the leaves.
Later: dusty fields under parched lilac mountains
and clumps of what must have been eucalyptus
by the peeling skin of their barks. I saw your face,
I saw your flesh in theirs, my suffering brother;
jacaranda over the streets, all looking broken,
as if all Mexico had this film of dust,
and between trees dotting the plain, fog,
thick as your clogged breath, shrouding the ranges
of, possibly, Santa de Something. I read this.
March 11. 8:35 a.m. Guadalajara, Saturday.
Roddy. Toronto. Cremated today.
The streets and trees of Mexico covered with ash.
Your soul, my twin, keeps fluttering in my head,
a hummingbird, bewildered by the rafters,
barred by a pane that shows a lucent heaven.
The maid sings behind the house,
with wooden clips in her teeth,
she rips down laundry like an avenging angel
and the hillside surges, sailing. Roddy.
Where are you this bright afternoon? I
am watching a soccer match listlessly
on TV, as you did sunk deep in the socket of the sofa,
your head shrunken, your eyes wet
and every exchange an ordeal.

II

I carry a small white city in my head,
one with its avenues of withered flowers,
with no sound of traffic but the surf,

no lights at dusk on the short street
where my brother and our mother live now
at the one address, so many are their neighbours!
Make room for the accommodation of the dead,
their mounds that multiply by the furrowing sea,
not in the torch-lit catacombs of your head
but by the almond-bright, spume-blown cemetery.
What was our war, veteran of threescore years and ten?
To save the salt light of the island
to protect and exalt its small people
to sit enthroned to a clicking scissors
watching the hot road and the blue flowers across it
and behind the hedge soft blue mountains
and the barber with the face of a boxer
say one who loves his craft more than a victory
not like that arrogantly tilted tailor of Moroni's
assessing you with the eyes of his scissors.

IV

When we were boys coming home from the beach,
it used to be such a thing! The body would be singing
with salt, the sunlight hummed through the skin
and a fierce thirst made iced water
a gasping benediction, and in the plated heat,
stones scorched the soles, and the cored dove hid
in the heat-limp leaves, and we left the sand
to its mutterings, and the long, cool canoes.

Threescore and ten plus one past our allotment,
in the morning mirror, the disassembled man.
And all the pieces that go to make me up—
the detached front tooth from a lower denture
the thick fog I cannot pierce without my glasses
the shot of pain from a kidney
these piercings of acute mortality.
And your wife, day and night,

assembling your accoutrements
to endure another day on the sofa,
bathrobe, glasses, teeth, because
your hands were leaves in a gust
when the leaves are huge veined, desiccated,
incapable of protest or applause.
To cedars, to the sea that cannot change its tune,
on rain-washed morning what shall I say then
to the panes reflecting the wet trees and clouds
as if they were storefronts and offices, and
in what voice, since I now hear changing voices?
The change of light on a pink plaster wall
is the change of a culture—how the light is seen,
how it is steady and seasonless in these islands
as opposed to the doomed and mortal sun of midsummer
or in the tightening circle of shadow in the bullring.
This is how a people look at death
and write a literature of gliding transience
as the sun loses its sight, singing of islands.

Sunrise then, the uncontaminated cobalt
of sky and sea. The hours idle, and I,
watching the heaving plumes of the palmistes
in the afternoon wind, I hear the dead sighing
that they are still too cold in the ochre earth
in the sun's sadness, to the caterpillar's accordion
and the ancient courtship of the turtle-doves.
Yellow-billed egret balanced on a black bull
its sheen so ebony rust shines through the coat
as the bamboos translate the threshing of the olives
as the olives the bamboo's calligraphy
a silvery twitter of a flock of fledglings
stuttering for rain, wires of a drizzle,
tinfoil of the afternoon sea and the dove's bassoon.
The house on the hill opposite—
blond beams criss-cross their shadows on grey stone,
finical, full of false confidence, then
a surge of happiness, inexplicable content,

like the light on a golden garden outside Florence,
afternoon wind resilvering the olives
and the sea's doves, white sails
and the fresh elation of dolphins
over the staghorn coral.
Cartagena, Guadalajara,
whose streets, if one eavesdropped,
would speak their demotic Castilian
if dust had not powdered the eucalyptus with silences
on the iron balcony's parenthesis
and the Aztec mask of Mercedes
on the tip of the tongue like a sparrow
dipping into the pool
and flicking its tail like a signature, a name
like the fluttering of wings in a birdbath—
Santiago de Compostela!

13

Flare of the flame tree and white egrets stalking.
Small bridge, brown trace, the new fire station.
And the clatter of parrots at sunrise
and at dusk their small wild souls returning
to the darkening trees, the pouis
against the Santa Cruz hills, orange and vermilion.
And great cities receding, Madrid, Genoa,
and their aisles with soaring arches
in the naves of shadow, the bamboo's basilica
the pillars of palmistes, Doric and Corinthian,
no, the point is not comparison or mimicry
in the incantations of fronds, nor the wafer-receiving
palms of the breadfruit, it is not in the envy
of hazed hills jealous of snow, not in the
pliant, surrendering lances of the cane
at Breda, not the indigo ignorance
that the ridges contain, because in what language
should the white herons talk, and with whose anger
do the wild parrots scream, who has tormented them
as mercilessly as we have tortured ourselves
with our conflicts of origins? Fill
the vessel of the egret with oblivious milk
and drink to the amnesia of Asia
with its yellow beaker, and listen, this time
to the correcting imprecations of the high palms:
"You are all mistaken, that is not what we are saying,
our prayers are not for you, there is nothing imperial
in our plumes, not for the horsemen of Bornu,
and the shells have no secret, and all your pages flutter
with the hysteria of parrots. Listen, we have
no envy of the white mountains, or of the white horn
above the smothered inns, no envy of the olive
or redoubtable oaks. We were never emblems.

The dawn would be fresh, the morning bliss,
if the light would break on your glaucous eyes
to see us without a simile, not just the green world
or streams where the pebbles are parables
and a plank bridge less than the Ponte Vecchio
or the motley of cocoa, its jester's hues and tatters
less than the harlequins in that *Rigoletto*
which elated you in Parma, or the slow haze of rain
that dried on the salty esplanade of Pescara,
or the darkness of Bosnia in the clouds of Santa Cruz.
The inheritance which you were sent to claim
defined itself in contradiction; there in that hall
among those porcelain-pink and dour burghers
was an illegitimate ancestor, as equal
as the African fishing through tall river-reeds
to pierce you, threshing on his stick."

II

And the first voice replied in the foam:
"What is culture if not the horizontal light
of magnificent gardens, statues dissolving in dusk
and fountains whose jets repeat an immortal phrase
to you, vague pilgrim? In long halls,
in incredible colonnades, the busts and portraits
will exist even if they were not looked at, perspectives
indifferent to your amazement. What is immortal
is what does not need your presence to assess it,
including these lines, even if you were never
disenchanted by the weather in Santiago de Compostela
or the mischievous drizzle on the dull esplanade
of banal Pescara, but you have caught an illness:
the malaria of dusk whose statues never shiver
or cough in the cold, or tremble with influential aspens,
and you will die from this indifference;
the horn of the white mountain above Zermatt
has gored you, and the lamps shine like blood drops

and the mantle rapidly climbs shrouding the snow
when memory blows out its candle
you can feel Europe drawn slowly over your cold brow."

III

So has it come to this, to have to choose?
The chafe of the breakers' moving marbles,
their lucent and commodious statuary
of turbulent stasis, changing repetition
of drizzling spray that glazes your eyes
like the marble miracles of the Villa Borghese?
Do not diminish in my memory
villages of absolutely no importance,
the rattling bridge over the stone-bright river,
un-ornate churches, chapels in the provinces
of light-exhausted Europe. Hoard, cherish
your negligible existence, your unrecorded history
of unambitious syntax, your clean pools
of unpolluted light over close stones.

15

I

Ritorno a Milano, if that's correct.
Past the stalagmites of the Duomo
the peaches of summer are bouncing
on the grids of the Milanese sidewalks
in halters cut close to the coccyx.
I look and no longer sigh for the impossible,
panting over a cupidinous coffee
like an old setter that has stopped chasing pigeons
up from the piazza. The skirts fly from me
without actual levitation, the young waiter
scrapes the crumbs of my years from the tablecloth.

Old man coming through the glass, who are you?
I am you. Learn to acknowledge me,
the cottony white hair, the heron-shanks,
and, when you and your reflection bend,
the leaf-green eyes under the dented forehead,
do you think Time makes exceptions, do you think
Death mutters, "Maybe I'll skip this one"?
the same silent consequence that crept across
your brother perilously sleeping, and all the others
whose silence is no different from your brother's.

There is an old man standing in the door glass there,
silent beyond raging, beyond bafflement,
past faith, whose knees easily buckle,
toothless at sunrise with white knotted hair,
who sometimes feels his flesh cold as the stone
that he will lie under, there where the sea-almonds
blaze in drought, and where a radiant sea
in an inexplicable exultation
exclaims its joy, and where the high cemetery
of marble clouds moves ponderously, lightly,

as if that were a heaven for old men
where those who have left await him,
cities of clouds and ghosts and whatever they mean.
All of the questions tangle in one question.
Why does the dove moan or the horse shake its mane?
Or the lizard wait on the white wall then is gone?

16

II

A grey dawn, dun. Rain-gauze shrouding the headlands.
A rainbow like a bruise through cottony cumuli.
Then, health! Salvation! Sails blaze in the sun.
A twin-sailed shallop rounding Pigeon Island.
This line is my horizon.
I cannot be happier than this.

II

Compare Milan, compare a glimpse of the Arno,
with this river-bed congealed with rubbish.
I have seen Venice trembling in the sun,
shadow-shawled Granada and the cork groves of Spain,
across the coined Thames, the grey light of London,
the drizzles sweeping Pescara's esplanade
and stone dolphins circling the basin of a fountain,
but, on the sloping pastures behind Gros Piton,
in the monumental shadow of that lilac mountain,
I have seen the terrestrial paradise.
And why waste all that envy when they take
as much pride in their suffering as in their cathedrals,
a vanity indifferent to proportions?
I have seen me shift from empire to empire;
I should have known that I would wind up beached
as I began on the blazing sand
rejected by the regurgitating billows
retreating with their long contemptuous hiss
for these chaotic sentences of seaweed
plucked by the sandpiper's darting concentration.
Be the one voice; the white Alps and the lace
of blossoms blown past the hotel window
or the leaves from the train window where you sat
through which you saw the ghost that is now your face
the poui's petals in the street lights of Zermatt.

O Altitudino! And my fear of heights.
But in Zermatt it was the clear, dry cold
that is the delight of skiers and of angels
over riven crevices where the old snow was packed
and the new snow almost blinded. Not different,
the one celestial, real geography.

III

We were headed steadily into the open sea.
Immeasurable and unplummetable fathoms
too deep for sounding or for any anchor,
the waves quick-running, crests, we were between
the pale blue phantoms of Martinique and St. Vincent
on the iron rim of the ringing horizon;
the farther we went out, the white bow drumming,
plunging and shearing spray, the wider my fear,
the whiter my spume-shot cowardice, as the peaks
receded, rooted on their separating world,
diminishing in the idea of home, but still the prow
pressed stubbornly through the gulfs and the helmsman
kept nodding in their direction through the glass
between the front deck and the wheel, their direction
meaning what we could not see but he knew was there
from talking on the radio to the other boat
that lay ahead of us towards which we plunged
and droned, a white slip of another smaller cruiser,
convinced by his smiling that we would breach them soon.
"Dolphins," the steersman said. "You will see them playing,"
but this was widening into mania, there were only
the crests that looked to their leaping, no fins,
no arching backs, no sudden frieze, no school today,
but the young captain kept on smiling, I had never
seen such belief in legend, and then, a fin-hint!
not a crest, and then splaying open under the keel
and racing with the bow, the legend broke water
and was reborn, her screams of joy
and my heart drumming harder, and the pale blue islands
were no longer phantom outlines, and the elate spray
slapped our faces with joy, and everything came
back as it was between the other islets, but
those with our own names, sometimes a fin

shot up, sometimes a back arched and re-entered
the racily running waves under which they glanced;
I saw their wet brown bodies gunning seaward,
more brown than golden despite the name "dorado,"
but I guess in the wet light their skins shone
too raw, too quiet to be miraculous,
too strange to quiet my fear, the skittering fish
from the first line of the open page, held
and held until the school was lost, the prodigal's home
was the horizon while my own peaks
loomed so inconsolably again, the roads, the roofs
of Soufrière in the wet sunlight. I watched them come.

IV

I had gaped in anticipation of an emblem
carved at a fountain's pediment from another sea
and when the dolphins showed up and I saw them
they arched the way thoughts rise from memory.
They shot out of the glacial swell like skiers
hurtling themselves out of that Alpine surf
with its own crests and plungings, spuming slopes
from which the dolphins seraphically soared
to the harps of ringing wires and humming ropes
to which my heart clung and those finished hopes
that I would see you again, my twin, "my dolphin."
And yet elation drove the dolphins' course
as if both from and to you, their joy was ours.
And had there been a prophecy that said: "Wait!
On a day of great delight you will see dolphins."
Or, in the ashes and embers of a wrecked sunset
the same voice, falling as quietly as a flag, said,
before the constellations arranged their chaos,
"Those drifting cinders are angels, see how they soar,"
I would not have believed in them, being too old
and sceptical from the fury of one life's
determined benedictions, but they are here.

Angels and dolphins. The second, first.
And always certainly, steadily, on the bright rim
of the world, getting no nearer or nearer, the more
the bow's wedge shuddered towards it, prodigal,
that line of light that shines from the other shore.